BREAKING the BONDS of Wickedness in the Last Days

How to Release Your Past and Embrace Your Future

Obii Pax-Harry

© Copyright 2007 - Obii Pax-Harry

All rights reserved. This book is protected under the copyright laws. This book may not be copied or reprinted for commercial gain or profit. The use of short quotations or occasional page copying for personal or group study is permitted and encouraged. Permission will be granted upon request. Scripture quotations are taken from the New King James Version of the Bible. Copyright © 1982 by Thomas Nelson. Used by permission. All rights reserved. Please note that Destiny Image Europe's publishing style capitalizes certain pronouns in Scripture that refer to the Father, Son, and Holy Spirit, and may differ from some Bible publishers' styles.

Take note that the name satan and related names are not capitalized. We choose not to acknowledge him, even to the point of violating grammatical rules.

DESTINY IMAGE EUROPE™ srl
Via Maiella, 1
66020 San Giovanni Teatino (Ch) - Italy

"Changing the world, one book at a time."

This book and all other Destiny Image Europe™ books are available at Christian bookstores and distributors worldwide.

To order products, or for any other correspondence, please contact:

DESTINY IMAGE EUROPE™ srl
Via Acquacorrente, 6
65123 - Pescara - Italy
Tel. +39 085 4716623 - Fax: +39 085 4716622
E-mail: info@eurodestinyimage.com

Or reach us on the Internet: **www.eurodestinyimage.com**

ISBN-13: 978-88-89127-43-8

For Worldwide Distribution. Printed in Italy.

1 2 3 4 5 6 7 8/10 09 08 07

Dedication

This book is dedicated first to the Holy Spirit, the Spirit of truth.

To my family—Chinyere Ukpabi-Asika, Apostle E. Ordu, Pastor Ogechi Ordu, and Prophetess Ngozi Nnadi—thanks for preparing me for my future.

To Rod and Julie Anderson, C. Peter Wagner, Cindy Jacobs, Chuck Pierce, Martin Scott, Emeka Nwankpa, Roger and Sue Mitchell, Dr. Paula Price, Geroge Otis, Jr., and Alistair Petri—you are a few of those people who have contributed to my spiritual development directly and indirectly through teachings, writings, and lifestyle. Thank you especially for your faithful contributions to the subjects of prophetic prayer and strategic levels of spiritual warfare.

Acknowledgments

I would like to thank Faye Burnett, friend and co-laborer, for enduring our experiences in Swaziland. I also would like to thank the warriors and faithful watchmen of Strategic Prayer School, now Birmingham House of Prayer, England, for exploring the realms with me. Finally, thanks to all at Resurrection Life Assembly, Birmingham, England, a praying church; I appreciate you and thank you for trusting me with your destinies.

May Heaven's gates remain attentive to the calls of the righteous!

Endorsements

Obii is a tenderhearted woman with a mischievous sense of humour and a wonderful love of people! It is into this context that she tackles the issues surrounding the bonds and snares that squeezes the life blood out of so many of our lives. Her love of life and the freedom that the Holy Spirit gives flows through every chapter. So a must for all you freedom fighters!

Steve Lowton
Apostolic/prophetic Leader in Europe
Leeds, UK

I have watched Obii's apostolic/prophetic gifting develop over the years with keen interest. My observation of the integrity of her heart and ministry, and more importantly, balance in her articulation of necessary revelation with which the Church is to advance in the days ahead, leads me to recommend this book as a must-read. Obii speaks of a realm she is familiar with, arming readers with divine wisdom to put to test insight she shares with passion.

Paul Adefarasin
Author, International Conference Speaker,
Founder of House On The Rock Churches,
Tele-Evangelist, Lagos, Nigeria

Obii is a dear friend of mine, and I warmly commend both her apostolic/prophetic ministry and also her new book, *Breaking the Bonds of Wickedness in the Last Days*. I concur with her comments that worship of the Lord must be placed at the forefront of a call to spiritual warfare. It is from this posture of humility that strategic spiritual warfare may be engaged in by divine prompt of the Holy Spirit and with Christ at the center. Obii's book is rich in wisdom and you will find it a riveting and revelatory read.

Catherine Brown
Author and Founder of Gatekeepers Global Ministries
http://www.gatekeepers.org.uk/

Table of Contents

	Foreword 11
	Introduction 15
Chapter 1	Why We Must Pray 19
Chapter 2	The Hour of Power 23
Chapter 3	Uncovering Familiar Patterns 39
Chapter 4	Binding the Strongman......................47
Chapter 5	Mind-set for the Days Ahead 51
Chapter 6	Breaking the Two-Year Cycle 57
Chapter 7	Unmasking Demonic Agents 61
Chapter 8	Breaking Familiar Patterns 65
Chapter 9	Setting the Captives Free 71

Prayer Shield

Introduction 77

Prayer Section 1	Spiritual War	83
Prayer Section 2	The Battle Belongs to the Lord	95
Prayer Section 3	Dressed for War	101
Prayer Section 4	The Weapon of the Word of God	107
Prayer Section 5	The Weapon of the Blood of Jesus	111
Prayer Section 6	The Weapon of the Believer's Authority	119
Prayer Section 7	The Weapon of His Name	122
Prayer Section 8	Break the Power of Fear	126
Prayer Section 9	Establish Boundaries	130
Prayer Section 10	Set Yourself Free	137
Prayer Section 11	Disarm the Enemy	144
Prayer Section 12	Defeat the Enemy	149
Prayer Section 13	Spiritual Enemies	155
Prayer Section 14	Engage With Angelic Forces	165
Prayer Section 15	Evil Communication Systems	168
Prayer Section 16	Present-Day Wars of the Church	172
Prayer Section 17	God Has a Hedge Around You	177
Prayer Section 18	Releasing Divine Blessings	180

Foreword

Obii has been my good friend for several years, and Rod, my husband, and I treasure her. From the moment I met her, I felt love for her. I was impressed that she had a strong call on her life to flow with prophetic prayer and that she would follow it. In her presence, there is a genuine and authentic sense that she has spent time with God, listening, hearing, and obeying His leading. We have seen how her spiritual life and natural life continue to grow, and it is a privilege to pray for her and witness her obeying God as she pioneers new ground.

Obii's writing flows in a depth and clarity of communication. She addresses foundational issues of evil that can be changed through apostolic declarations. Yet a young believer can dive into this book and learn much from the experiences that Obii has been allowed to journey through.

Through this wonderful new book, she brings a challenge to all those who want to break wickedness off their own lives and stand in the gap for others. You will learn that praying is the way to win spiritual battles, and to pray aloud with expectancy and hope in order to experience lasting change in challenging circumstances.

The prayers, when prayed from the heart, really do release dynamic power. While we all can sense coalitions of evil strengthening themselves together in these end days, we know there is a righteous army being awakened—pure-hearted believers who are seriously committed to face today's evil in a solid united front.

Many new intercessors are being raised up and trained to spiritually steward their cities under Holy Spirit-inspired strategies.

The Body of Christ is being called to rise up to a fuller measure and stature of Jesus Christ. There is a call to a fresh accountability on new levels to pray for cities, nations, and continents. We live in exciting and challenging days, when we must understand what it means to maintain what is being obtained.

While there are other great books that include prayers for spiritual warfare and breaking bondages off our lives, this book, *Breaking the Bonds of Wickedness in the Last Days*, speaks clearly to our need to understand this new move of God, and be made ready.

In Obii's own words, the forerunner views in this book are written out of her conviction and focus on how to face the emerging spiritual trends of our time. This book offers the reader many practical and brilliant ideas on how to build a prayer shield and pray victory prayers. It will encourage your heart and enlighten your mind to the reality of the present-day wars that the Body of Christ faces and prepare you for spiritual victory.

Obii has lived what she has written in this book. Her disclosures on spiritual warfare after midnight in the Western world will help prepare you as a believer and train you how to receive a breakthrough. Yes, Obii, you have stated it well in saying that "God is raising up a people who know the score!" I pray that many people read this book and are armed with the insights and strengths that are exposed in these powerful pages, which destroy the unrighteous foundations that attract sin.

Julie Anderson
Co-Founder, Prayer For the Nations, and
Strategic Prayer Schools, UK,
Founder of Deborah Company UK

Introduction

The book in your hands was birthed out of a personal and corporate experience unimaginable to the civilized mind. We as believers in Christ Jesus, the Author and Finisher of our faith, are not to fear the spiritual wars of our time (see Matt. 24:6). Furthermore, forerunning views expressed by a recognized apostle of distinction in a book on territory-taking is worth more than a flickering attention. C. Peter Wagner wrote in the 1990's, "As we enter the kingdom of God we can choose one of two postures. We can draw back and protect ourselves in a defensive posture or we can move forward aggressively in an offensive posture."[1] *Breaking the Bonds of Wickedness in the Last Days* can be said to have emanated from a conscious yet humble decision to choose the latter view. I strongly believe the Church needs to adopt an offensive posture in the spiritual wars of our time.

I have written out of commission and conviction on two levels: first, to draw attention to emerging spiritual trends, and second, to offer in humility a radical prayer shield. I give glory to the Lord for inspiring a prayer section in this book through which revolutionary suggestions have been offered. Each section contains victory prayers learned at the feet of Jesus and then applied by me and others to real-life experiences. Our overcoming testimonies, which are told indirectly through the same prayers, have achieved desired results, and will encourage your heart and enlighten your mind to the reality of present-day spiritual wars.

As said, my aim in writing is not to simply draw attention to *emerging spiritual trends* of evil that the Church cannot afford to ignore; but the heart of this divine assignment is to put before the saints suggestions to areas of concern that have been highlighted.

The prayers in this book are scriptural and are to be taken seriously. They are to be prayed aloud with *expectancy* and *hope* to experience lasting change in challenging circumstances. A man or woman who prays to the living God without faith or hope for answers to requests made may negate their mission.

In answer to a request to teach His disciples how to pray, Jesus said, "*When you pray, say...*" (see Luke 11:2a, emphasis added), and not "if" you pray. In addition, prayer said without faith will birth hopelessness. The Bible reminds us that Abraham our forefather "*contrary to hope, in hope believed*" (Rom. 4:18a). "*Hope does not disappoint*" (Rom. 5:5a), because our hope comes from God who "*is a rewarder of those who diligently seek Him*" (Heb. 11:6b). Prayer is the way a child of God wins spiritual battles. As you read and pray the prayers in this book, you will experience a new level of authority in your prayer life. The Bible also makes clear that "*the effective, fervent prayer of a righteous man avails much*" (James 5:16b). The spiritual wars in this endtime can be won only with radical holiness on the part of believers who also must pray.

No matter the systems, methods, or options that are available to believers, prayer to my mind is still the only way a child of God overcomes opposition to the divine will of God for his or her life (see Jer. 29:12).

Jesus Christ continued to encourage His disciples to pray, as noted in the following Scripture: "*Then He spoke a parable to them, that*

Introduction

men always ought to pray and not lose heart" (Luke 18:1). He also encouraged His disciples to confront the demonic with faith in order to save others from oppression (see Matt. 17:18-20). With some forms of demon possession, as I mention in this book, Jesus taught that *"this kind does not go out except by prayer and fasting"* (Matt. 17:21). The Lord's teaching appears to suggest that it is necessary to employ different levels of prayer in relation to prevailing demonic oppositions. Prayer and fasting are a necessary combination in evicting demonic occupants of lives, cities, nations, and even continents.

My experience and the experience of others during a season of warfare, which was a short but intense span of time, armed me with insight and strength to compile the information you presently have in your hands. I have also included materials from other credible experts on the subject of spiritual warfare, a clear reflection of the progressive nature of revelation. Several years ago, the Holy Spirit informed me that there would be a time when the writing and experiences of others would be advanced by younger ministries in a relay, race-team type of experience. Christian soldiers are not to fear the spiritual wars of our time, but to consider them as part of personal and corporate journeys to new levels of spiritual growth. In recognition of this divine truth, the apostle Paul declared, *"Therefore we do not lose heart. Even though our outward man is perishing, yet the inward man is being renewed day by day"* (2 Cor. 4:16).

May the Lord bless you as you read and as you pray.

Obii Pax-Harry

Endnote

1. C. Peter Wagner, *Territorial Spirits* (Tonbridge, Kent: Sovereign World, 1991) p. 5.

CHAPTER 1

Why We Must Pray

It is extremely important to remind oneself that the processes of life are generally to be seen as stepping-stones for future accomplishments. Hence, the Bible urges believers to *"...count it all joy when you fall into various trials, knowing that the testing of your faith produces patience"* (James 1:2-3). However, when your focus is cast on the trials, your eyes will register a counter report. A negative report from ten spies compromised Israel's journey to the Promised Land (see Num. 13:32-33).

Moreover, patience in itself, if undisturbed, achieves divine purpose as the next verse assures: *"But let patience have its perfect work, that you may be perfect and complete, lacking nothing"* (James 1:4). I cannot claim to have become complete and mature, lacking nothing, but I am compelled by the Lord to give "such as I have" (see Acts 3:6) by way of my testimony entitled, *Breaking the Bonds of Wickedness in the Last Days.*

IGNORANCE IS NO EXCUSE

Before I lived through the bulk of the experience that formed a foundation for this book, I had felt spiritual warfare was not for me, as do many other believers. My personal philosophy on the subject matter made sense to me, except that it was founded on a comfortable foundation called "ignorance." I had a sense of the Lord's continual grace and mercy, but did not realize I was expected to partner with Heaven on destiny issues. Growing up in Nigeria, I read of and heard accounts of witchcraft in local newspapers and magazines but was never personally exposed to the stories I considered weird. I later moved to Britain in my teenage years and attended a Church of England boarding school. I was sent to a "Christian nation" that was once a colonial master of the nation I was born at. My normal life was exciting enough with no need for accounts of the devil's ploys. However, as I grew up in the Lord, answering the call of God on my life, nothing prepared me for the reality of spiritual activities after midnight in the Western world.

Ignorance is not a defense under common law burden of proof, and neither does it provide protection in spiritual matters. Indeed, the Bible warns us that *"My people are destroyed for lack of knowledge"* (Hos. 4:6a). Ignorance leads to mental and physical captivity as the Bible also points out: *"Therefore My people have gone into captivity, because they have no knowledge"* (Isa. 5:13a). Furthermore, ignorance, which is synonymous with spiritual blindness, can lead to lawlessness as the Word of God also emphasizes. Without revelation, people act according to their own will, to satisfy the lust of the flesh—*"Where there is no revelation, the people cast off restraint"* (Prov. 29:18a).

So, it is the responsibility of believers to appropriate benefits of the Word of God and to order their lives therein. A fresh revelation from our covenant-keeping God is necessary for the Body of Christ. It is important that every believer soldier understands present-day wars of the Church. This is necessary if we are to dethrone false ideologies and occult practices. It is upon demonic thrones of iniquity that satanic rules are established and used to challenge destinies and purposes of God.

THE WORD AND THE SPIRIT

As I mentioned previously, the primary purpose of this writing is to awaken the Church to emerging spiritual trends capable of challenging our steadfastness and responsibilities to the world (see Ps. 125:3). In reality, many believers are struggling to make sense of their spiritual journey in everyday experiences and otherwise, while the Word of God is clear about God's desire and heart for His children. However, some of life's experiences challenge a much needed balance between the Word and the Spirit. In emphasizing the need for harmony between understanding of Scripture and Holy Spirit-inspired experiences, Martin Scott wrote:

> Spirit-inspired experience must illuminate Scripture. Our beliefs and practices need to fall within the boundaries of Scripture, but careful reflection on or experience must be brought to Scripture so its pages become illuminated in fresh ways.[1]

Unless we examine our lives before the Lord honorably and humbly, we will stand no chance before the accuser of the brethren. The prayers contained in this book are fundamental to establishing *righteous foundations* in the lives of believers (see 1 Pet. 4:10). They are for no other purpose but to prepare believers for fresh impetus to fulfill our mandates as stewards on the earth. And as stewards, we are required to stand pure before the Lord.

Each section of prayers has been inspired by the Holy Spirit's guidance in a time when I needed to learn a new prayer language to overcome demonic forces that challenged my destiny. As already mentioned, the prayers are biblical and are founded on the Word of God (see Isa. 55:10-11). Many people have received a turnaround in their circumstances just by working through the prayer shield even in its infant stage. It is my prayer that you too will receive your divine breakthrough. Whatever you put into prayer will render you the results you deserve (see Jer. 33:3).

The Bible reminds every believer of the reward for prayer. "*The effective, fervent prayer of a righteous man avails much*" (James 5:16). Satan hates a praying Christian. So it is important for pressure to be applied in uprooting evil forces seeking to thwart destinies of believers. Apostolic-type prayers are often effective against demonic hierarchies, such as are identified in Ephesians 6:12: "*For we do not wrestle against flesh and blood, but against principalities, against powers, against the rulers of the darkness of this age, against spiritual hosts of wickedness in the heavenly places.*"

Ephesians chapter 6 reveals that there is a perverted authority festering in social structures, philosophies, and persuasions, as well as ruling in the compromised hearts of individuals. Both tenacity and consistency are key elements in effective praying to dislodge these demonic influences. The Bible warns, "*The end of all things is at hand; therefore be serious and watchful in your prayers*" (1 Pet. 4:7). As an anointed child of God, you are to call on the Lord with persistence until you receive your breakthrough (see Jer. 29:12), for the Lord's plans toward His children are good and perfect plans (see Jer. 29:11). He is Messiah, the Breaker who has broken doors and gates of opposition with His blood (see Micah 2:13). A person who seeks after the Lord with hope and in hope is never disappointed (see Prov. 23:18), and God is a rewarder of those who diligently seek Him (see Heb. 11:6).

Endnote

1. Martin Scott, *Sowing Seeds for Revival* (Tonbridge, Kent: Sovereign World, 2001) p. 30.

CHAPTER 2

The Hour of Power

The global spiritual climate is fast attracting the attention of believers and unbelievers alike. Cosmic upheavals of varying degrees have kept newscasters busy as nation after nation records disasters of disturbing magnitudes. In His teachings, the Lord Jesus highlighted several Scriptures pointing to the evil day now at hand (see Matt. 24), and the Body of Christ is to prepare for such a day that has been long prophesied.

Men will seek to pursue their evil lusts and desires, outworking deviousness in ways unimaginable, but believers in Christ are not to be unduly bothered. An important key to spiritual breakthrough lies in understanding, and revelation is closely linked with understanding. However, "seeing something by revelation is not enough—it must then be prayed through until we know that it is in process of release."[1]

For years I suffered numerous spiritual attacks capable of crushing the most mature spirit emotionally and spiritually. Fortunately, my innate gift of optimism made light of every hurdle placed by the enemy at close range to subvert me in my cause (see Lam. 3:35-37). The Lord trusts His children to go through certain "trials" for His glory. He is forever watching over His own (see Ps. 127:1). And at the end of every trial is a success story, often for the benefit of others who enjoy dividends of hard-won victories (see James 1:2). It is pertinent to note that the devil, using all manner of evil ploys, directs his deviousness at believers. His antics are not to be given room for expansion or multiplication; instead, they are to be nullified through violent prayers. God cannot be tempted by evil, nor does He tempt anyone (see James 1:13); rather, "various trials" are to be endured with joy. They often lead believers into positive ends so that they are *"mature and complete, not lacking anything"* (see James 1:4b). The Lord sometimes refines and tests His children *"in the furnace of affliction"* (Isa. 48:10b), but His afflictions are "light," possessing God-ordained purposes. They are *"working for us a far more exceeding and eternal weight of glory"* (2 Cor. 4:17). Hence, every affliction or trial cannot be attributed to the devil's ploys but are deserving of interpretation in order that appropriate response can be given.

THE DAY OF POWER

The psalmist wrote, *"Your people shall be volunteers in the day of Your power"* (Ps. 110:3a).

The day of God's power is also the day of His people's power—a day of power for the Church (see Dan. 7:22). Furthermore, because the devil works in the opposite of God's will, it means that in the day of God's power, he will also proudly claim power. Larry Lea's contribution by way of prophetic insight to the subject of strategic level spiritual warfare is worthy of mention. He writes:

> Today God is raising up a company of people who know what the score really is, where the action really is in God. They're aware that unclean spirits are roaming this earth, seeking places to dwell in order to destroy men and women.

The emerging company will have listening ears for what the Holy Spirit is saying to the church today, and they'll answer His call to battle. They know that this battle is a battle in the spirit realm, and they are ready for combat.[2]

The Church is God's Body on earth, and believers are His followers and representatives, who are to enforce God's Word in every aspect of life. God's Word is His testament, His judgment. Consider that when judgment is passed in a civil matter in a natural court of law (under common law jurisdictions), such judgment is ineffective until served on a defaulting party. In like manner, the Word of God, as an eternally valid judgment, will not lose its essence, but its judgments will be enforced against any counterfeits.

The apostle Paul teaches believers to pull down strongholds, which include, *"arguments and every high thing that exalts itself against the knowledge of God..."* (2 Cor. 10:5b). I sincerely believe the Church is in a dispensation of God's power and of His glory, which is to be transmitted and distributed throughout all the earth. Dispensational interpretation of the Church's experience in this present millennium may accord credence to my humble submission that the Church is in her day of power. If the opinion that the Church of the last day will ascend the realm of those who "overcome" through contentions is accepted, then hard times of the last few years qualify us to overcome by the blood of Jesus and testimonies ensuing (see Rev. 12:11).

PEOPLE OF POWER

Indeed, God's people shall be volunteers in His day of power. Transitioning to eternal reign of power from His incarnate nature, Jesus said, *"Nevertheless not My will, but Yours, be done"* (Luke 22:42b). Authority is the key to power.[3] God's power is poured into humble, selfless vessels, totally yielded to the divine will of the Father. It is with this same power of the Almighty God that false gods are to be dethroned (see Zech. 4:6-7). The early Church was constituted of volunteers in a day or age of God's power. Peter was so full of supernatural power that the Bible records, *"... they brought the sick out into the* streets and laid them on the beds and couches, that at least the shadow of Peter passing by might fall on some of them" (Acts 5:15). This was a time when even the shadow of a vessel filled with the Spirit of God could be relied on to heal the sick.

In our present times, holiness and transparency are two essential keys for accessing a dimension of God's nature to set captives free. It is a recorded fact that the power of God resident in Peter executed God's judgment against the demonic forces, challenging the health of those bound. Today, the anointing resident in the functions given to the Church by Christ in full operation (see Eph. 4:11-16) breaks yokes of the enemy. *"It shall come to pass in that day that his burden shall be taken away from your shoulder, and his yoke from your neck, and the yoke will be destroyed because of the anointing oil"* (Isa. 10:27).

The Body of Christ needs to rise to the stature Jesus Christ died to give us. Demonic coalitions are strengthening their cords of evil, but against a united righteous army they will stand no ground. The devil has sent messengers, strong principalities, and powers to stand against the Church, to keep believers from attaining all that God has preordained for us.[4] Therefore, if believers are to steward God's manifold wisdom and grace on the earth for the sake of the lost, then a need to understand emerging trends of evil cannot be overemphasized. Intercessors, for instance, need to understand the nature of cords that bind prevailing evil and if such cords have been loosened. In addition, it is important to carefully analyze foundations of evil in order to effectively demolish them through apostolic-type decrees (see Job 22:28).

My approach to spiritual warfare is undergirded by an overwhelming sense of responsibility as a steward of God's manifold grace. Martin Scott rightly points out, "There are diverse viewpoints on spiritual warfare and although there is a tendency to think that our views have been informed by a pure reading of Scripture, we need to acknowledge that the beliefs we subscribe to are in part dependent on our *world-view*."[5] He then goes on to define world-view as "something that will affect how we approach spiritual warfare. A *world-view* is the lens through which we see the world. It is the filter that our experiences go through in order to be interpreted. This lens or filter will shape the way we respond and live."6

Jesus was particular about the need to bind the strongman over territories in order to cast off the bonds of wickedness (see Luke 11:22-23; Matt. 12:29-30). The time has come to confront demonic foundations sabotaging the efforts of the Church and threatening advancement of the Kingdom. Larry Lea believes:

> Over some cities are spirits of avarice and greed. Over others are spirits of violence. Over still others are spirits of addiction. So the only thing that will change what is going on in our cities is an army of intercessors who will stand and raise their hands in prayer and praise to poke holes in the darkness.7

GAINING GROUND

The Lord recently spoke to me concerning cities, nations, and the Church. He spoke of territory-taking strategies. He whispered into my heart, "My people know how to *take* grounds, but many do not know how to *maintain* grounds gained."

In other words, the Church, through prayer, has the capacity to evict illegal occupants of spiritual climates, ranging from false ideologies to immoral acts. But prayers for the manifestation of God's Kingdom in cities and nations are not just casual seasonal events, but are to be sustained. I learned this lesson while leading a team from the then Strategic Prayer School to pray in the city of Birmingham, England toward a scheduled gay pride event. We called on the God of Elijah outside of a bar that exhibited blasphemous profanities. The ground outside this bar was anointed by direction from the leading of the Holy Spirit, as we called on the Lord to send down His fire. Our prayer of faith was targeted at the gateway to unrighteousness and not to humans.

I was amazed when one of my team members telephoned me with an amazing report. Ten days after our assignment, the particular bar we anointed was on the local news broadcast, having caught fire.

Thankfully, no one was injured. The God of Elijah did intervene as that bar was boarded off for a considerable length of time. However, I remember the Holy Spirit speaking clearly into my heart that it would take a "sustained attack" to keep the spirits behind the homosexual lifestyle out of our city.

Effective management of victories gained in the realm of the spirit means that we must revisit prayer topics, as a reminder of a need to press into the future. Unless past challenges are remembered and used as leverage for future gains, we will miss opportunities for growth. The Body of Christ needs to celebrate warfare victories in thanksgiving as a memorial to God.

The devil has his memory bank well structured in order to sustain an agenda of revisiting stronghold sites. Satan enjoys reminding people of past failures while blighting memories of victories. He is an accuser of the brethren (see Rev. 12:10). Jesus warned against the laid-back attitude that cause some to operate in the mind-set of a retreating army (see Matt. 12:43-45). Unless the Church sees the need to gain *and maintain* spiritual grounds, the risk of losing grounds, such as souls of men and women bound to sin, will be an unfortunate reality. As a member of God's army, your part in fulfilling the corporate commission of the Church requires that bonds of wickedness in your life or family line be broken. Once these bonds are broken, prevailing prayers serve to provide canopies of protection over spiritual territories previously held ransom by the strongman.

TAKING TERRITORIES FOR GOD

It is simply not enough to declare land-taking initiatives. The Church is required to make future plans, implementing strategies necessary to preserve spoils of spiritual battles. For instance, drug addicts who receive Jesus Christ as Lord, by becoming born again, are spiritual lands gained. However, unless discipleship programs run concurrently with rehabilitation regimes, such valuable lives or lands may be lost to the devil. As stewards of lands and God's manifold grace, the Church is to be light in our cities, transmitting hope in Christ to the lost in sin. The devil has never been given authority over the earth, even though he was cast down to earth with a host of fallen angels (see Isa. 14:12-17; Rev. 12:9). Rather, members of the Body of Christ are governors of God's manifold grace individually and corporately (see 1 Pet. 4:10). Yet our divine mandate as governors or stewards of lands has been the subject of contention since the fall of man. In the New Testament context, leaders in the Church and believers are referred to as stewards (see 1 Cor. 4:1; Titus 1:7; 1 Pet. 4:10), a greater responsibility from that of the first Adam who was required to take care of the ground.

The Greek word, *oikonomos*, translating "stewards" comes from two words—*oikos*, meaning "economy" and *nemo*, meaning to "arrange." The word originally referred to a manager of a house but in a wider sense refers to an administrator or a steward in general. A steward is a person in charge of a household, standing between the household and the owner with the responsibility of feeding the household. A steward is accountable to the owner for the dispensation of materials, goods, and services entrusted to him.

Likewise, the Church is accountable to God for cities, nations, and continents. So, it is important that intercessory armies are raised and trained as "watchmen" and stewards who administer God's unfailing love in their cities. Spiritual grounds repossessed from the enemy, such as souls of men regained from the clutches of darkness, may be contended by the same spirits that were evicted, unless necessary practical assistance is put in place. Holy Spirit-inspired programs should be implemented to steward their newfound freedom in Christ. Barbara Wentroble believes that "success, however, must be maintained. The enemy does not stop when he experiences a setback. He looks for an opportunity to gain ground once again." She says that "apostolic churches maintain alertness in the spirit" and should "not rest in past victories. These churches are always attentive for any openings to the enemy. Grateful for the entirety of what the Lord has done in the past, they press on until their lives and cities become praiseworthy."[8]

I have found this viewpoint to bear a heart resonance to my personal experience. With a mind-set of stewardship, I have felt better equipped mentally, spiritually, and physically to respond to Heaven's burdens for cities and nations. I can understand Paul's statement in Second Corinthians 5:14a, *"For the love of Christ compels us."* My focus has changed from being a victim to seeking understanding of root causes of evil around me. A key root cause revealed by the Holy Spirit surprisingly has been wickedness of the heart (see Jer. 17:9).

BURNING THE FLAME OF HOPE

The devil is unable to take off like a fighter jet to a target, except where war exists and a runway has been built through sin for that particular aircraft (see Prov. 26:2). So, unless pathways are constructed in the spirit realm through idolatry, satanic vehicles such as freemasonry, witchcraft, voodoo, homosexuality, or new age deception cannot take off or land.

Research into the history of lands, known also as spiritual mapping, plays an important role in rooting out evil. Unless unrighteous foundations that attract sin are destroyed, the light of Christ's Gospel will not shine to full illumination in our cities.

I remember having a vision during a prayer meeting in 2003 where I was literally transported in the spirit to the city council chambers of our city. There appeared to have been a consultative meeting regarding a symbol of hope in our city named, "the flame of hope"; and principalities and powers seeking to stake claims on our city were specifically targeting this symbol of Christianity. The Lord identified a man in a white shirt as a "lone voice" in the meeting. He was surrounded by many from other faiths and agnostics. We were commanded to pray for the lone voice and that the flame of hope would not be turned off due to shortage of funds.

I was amazed when the newspapers likewise reported that the city council was claiming lack of funding as an argument to turn off a clear symbol of Christianity in a strategic square, which had been revealed by the Lord as a source of power.[9] In answer to our prayers and the prayers of others, a businessman offered to pay the required sum of 16,000 pounds so that the flame of hope could keep burning. How important it is when the Church partners with Christ, when intercessors pray with hope.

The subject of spiritual warfare is one that has caused much argument, dissensions, and agreements alike. Some in the Body of Christ believe spiritual warfare is not for Christians. Their argument seems to suggest engaging in spiritual warfare may expose participants to unnecessary backlash or counterattack. However, I have come to believe that the mind-set with which a believer responds to spiritual challenges is extremely important. Commenting on existence of demonic activities in the invisible realm, C. Peter Wagner wrote:

> I embrace a high view of scripture that I come to the conclusion that spirit beings have personalities and names, that they think and talk, that they have wills and that they act on decisions they make. They are created by God, but they are not created in the image of God as human beings are. All this is clearly stated in both the Old Testament and the New Testament.[10]

In my humble experience, praying and interacting at certain levels of authority, I will submit to the views above and that of any others of the same persuasion. In addition, I choose to follow steps of a respected theologian and pioneer in the area of strategic level spiritual warfare, citing C.S. Lewis who comments:

> There are two equal and opposite errors into which our race can fall about the devils. One is to disbelieve in their existence. The other is to believe, and to feel an excessive and unhealthy interest in them.[11]

Martin Scott, another experienced prophet and one who has walked the roads of many nations in prayer, has expressed a view worthy of our note. He defines *spiritual warfare*:

> At the most basic levels spiritual warfare is simply living for Christ in the context of a hostile environment. Our environment is hostile being set against the work of God. The source

of that hostility is both external—the world system and the devil; and also internal—the flesh.[12]

The fact that all the Body of Christ do not share common views on the existence of an invisible realm and activities of invisible beings, should not deter those who respond to divine mandates to create awareness or stir further debates on such an important topic. The more experiences are shared, bizarre or not, to differing views, the more likely the reality of common ground. The existence of present-day spiritual wars of the Church needs to be communicated so that those who are to fight are prepared. An essential preparation process requires believers to break the bonds of wickedness, which may compromise spiritual authority of even the most experienced apostle. It is natural for people to question unfamiliar or unexplored spiritual grounds. Spirit beings, invisible realms, and angels are a few examples of unfamiliar terrains where great minds have parted ways due to a lack of common understanding. For instance, in Acts chapter 10, Peter the apostle revealed that his mind-set was trapped in Jewish expectations, as he was not entirely ready to accept the new dimension of ministry to the Gentiles.

FAITHFUL TO THE CAUSE

I firmly suggest that worship of the Almighty be placed at the forefront of a call to spiritual warfare. Our primary calling is to worship the Lord, and He is calling for worship on the earth in these last days (see John 4:23-24). Then strategic level spiritual warfare should be engaged in only by divine calling, with the Lord as the center of all activities.

I consider any time given to studying a defeated foe as time wasted, unless commissioned by God to do so. Hence, my commitment to strategic level spiritual warfare is in context of divine assignment. The Bible makes clear that the devil, our adversary, is an enemy, not a friend. Believers are warned to *"be sober, be vigilant; because your adversary the devil walks about like a roaring lion, seeking whom he may devour"* (1 Pet. 5:8). The devil confirmed this aimless, wandering evil nature when questioned by God on one occasion. God asked satan, *"From where do you come?" So satan answered the Lord and said, "From going to and fro on the earth, and from walking back and forth on it"* (Job 1:7). Satan also appeared before God to accuse Joshua's righteousness: *"Then he showed me Joshua the high priest standing before the Angel of the Lord, and satan standing at his right hand to oppose him"* (Zech. 3:1).

Satan, the devil, is still challenging the plans of God for all creation through the many trials believers face, which are contrary to their expectations. He achieves his plans using stumbling blocks, such as sickness or unemployment, to hinder a person's preordained purpose. For example, a believer may have his faith shaken by a diagnosis of cancer or become depressed when he loses a job. Satan constantly recycles past challenges because he is barren and incapable of conception. In addition, through emotional upheavals caused by circumstances, which may not be wholly spiritual, satan uses mind games to hold his victims hostage. The mind may then be plagued by accusation of unworthiness. It is to be remembered that the devil does not accuse the righteousness of a new creation in Christ (see 2 Cor. 5:17); rather, he seeks to accuse the righteousness of Christ in you. He knows your righteousness outside of the blood of Jesus Christ is as filthy rags, and vulnerable to the devil's challenges (see Isa. 1:18). Hence, we are to put on Christ as an outer garment—*"But put on the Lord Jesus Christ, and make no provision for the flesh, to fulfill its lusts"* (Rom. 13:14).

Joshua in the Old Testament was a pattern of a new creation believer in Christ, being cleansed from sin—*"...old things have passed away; behold, all things have become new"* (2 Cor. 5:17). Our sins have been wiped away in the blood of Jesus (see Heb. 9:22), and it will take renewed minds in Christ to walk free from demonic oppression. Believers in Christ will suffer much in the spiritual wars of our time unless the bonds of the wickedness of this age are broken.

PREVAILING SIN

Because satan is unable to subvert or thwart divinely ordained purposes, he deceives people into living in their own righteousness rather than the inherited righteousness in Christ Jesus, which releases grace to live victoriously. As the Bible reminds us, "*...all have sinned and fall short of the glory of God*" (Rom. 3:23). Satan thrives in accusing the brethren.

Prevailing sin or persistent strongholds in a spiritual climate, such as homosexuality, may compromise inhabitants, including Christians, as was the case with biblical Sodom. A life of sin translates to slavery, mocking the sacrifice of the life of Jesus. A person who opts for a lifestyle of sin compromises his or her authority to war against a satanic stronghold. As a slave, he pays dues to his master and loses the right to battle against his captor.

> *Do you not know that to whom you present yourselves slaves to obey, you are that one's slaves whom you obey, whether of sin leading to death, or of obedience leading to righteousness?* (Romans 6:16)

Many people in our societies presently struggle with all manner of addictions. They are habitual sinners who are slaves to sin, having abandoned the grace given through the blood of Jesus, which breaks the bonds of wickedness that enslaves souls. Sin is of the devil and is ruled by the devil, and the consequence of sin leads to spiritual death as the Bible warns: "For the wages of sin is death" (Rom. 6:23). Sin opens doors through which the devil strikes at a believer's life (see James 4:7). So, the Word of God warns:

> *For the scepter of wickedness shall not rest on the land allotted to the righteous, lest the righteous reach out their hands to iniquity* (Psalm 125:3).

The Church retains the mandate to watch over cities and nations as the Scripture above recommends, and the devil understands that as a child of God, you have power to overcome temptations—"*For sin shall not have dominion over you, for you are not under law but under grace*" (Romans 6:14). But instead of embracing the free gift of grace for repentance, some within the Body of Christ are deceived by satan into the pride of sinning. Furthermore, a born-again believer can be vulnerable to evil when there is sin in a heart. For instance, a born-again believer in Christ may come from a family line with members yet involved in idolatry, satanic worship, or clear-cut initiated witchcraft. Such a believer will remain a target for spirits with specific assignments to maintain family altars. Through sacrifices offered at specific times, family deities are appeased, and any time a child of God falls victim to these spirits, the effect is similar to offering a sacrifice. Emeka Nwankpa, a recognized African apostle of prayer, writes:

> The covenants men make with these spirits draw such people into sorcery, witchcrafts, enchantments, soothsaying, divination, necromancy, astrology, libations, sacrifices, feasts, and festivals.[13]

Foundations of unrighteousness may compromise a believer's destiny. Ananias and his wife, Sapphira, are one such biblical example of the consequences of unrighteousness in the heart. They were bonded in a marriage covenant, which stood on an unrighteous foundation of greed, and their lust for money led to eventual consecutive death (see Acts 5:1-11). Lot's wife disobeyed instructions from the angels of the Lord that were sent to destroy Sodom. She looked back at the city she loved, despite the prevailing sin of that city, and as a result, she turned into a pillar of salt (see Gen. 19:26). She was attracted to an unrighteous foundation due to unrighteousness in her own heart. Compromise in the heart of Lot's wife made her love what God hated (see Num. 25:3-4; Ps. 106:19-20). Unless efforts are made to renounce and sever allegiances to family idols, access will be given to such idols to seek harvests at appointed times.

It is not enough to recite the sinner's prayer and then hope for the best. Public renunciation of ties to idols and family or community deities is crucial to a believer's sustained victorious life. A believer in Christ Jesus cannot serve two masters at a time. Elijah challenged the children of Israel who were captivated with Baal worship saying, *"How long will you falter between two opinions? If the Lord is God, follow Him; but if Baal, follow him"* (1 Kings 18:21b).

As I have mentioned, unrighteous foundations serve as landing strips for numerous demonic alliances. Familiar spirits, for instance, who serve as satanic surveillance agents responsible for the *department of deception*, thrive on such foundations. I shall expound on activities of these present-day enemies of the Church in succeeding chapters. It is these spirits that sustain a family's allegiance to idols and demonic foundations.

In a recent case of severe witchcraft attacks that I and others were subjected to, I was forced into a level of consecrated and sanctified prayer, which I never imagined myself capable of. I sought the face of the Lord in prayer, seeking to understand the possibility of church-attending Christians becoming involved in demonic activities, albeit innocently. It was important to me to understand ways in which active Christians may yield to demands of generational witchcraft or idolatry and idol worshipping. I had been exposed to teachings of theologians who argued that born-again believers cannot become demon possessed. I do not dispute their teaching, but I do not agree with the principles upon which such teachings are based. I desire, rather, to remain faithful to boundaries of understanding I have been privileged to receive.

I truly believe an important aspect of our theology needs to consider the enemy's means of transporting witchcraft. How is it possible that a person who lives in Sweden can be contacted by familiar spirits from his family line in Mongolia? Believers commonly state, *"There is no distance in the spirit."* So, because the devil copies, clones, and mimics Heaven's plans, can one conclude that *"there is no distance in the spirit for evil"*? When Christians complain about demonic oppression and spiritual warfare, should they be seen as victims of wild imaginations, or can the devil still affect spiritual climates as the *"prince of the power of the air"*? (see Eph. 2:2). Are the victims of sin who are referred to as *"sons of disobedience"* (see Eph. 2:2), simply stiff-necked, sin-loving vagrants, or victims of demonic manipulation? These are some of the thoughts I intend to provoke to stages of conscious analysis.

ANALYZING THE TRENDS

At the beginning of the 1990s, C. Peter Wagner wrote, "Through recent decades God has been moving His people, step by step, through phases of preparation, setting the agenda for the current decade. *As I analyze the trends...."*[14]

I personally commend a man who has perceived a need to analyze emerging trends for a decade. I feel a heart alignment with his mission, recognizing I was within the ambit of reason when my heart answered, *"Here am I! Send me"* (Isa. 6: 8b).

A thorough study on *emerging trends* of evil, following after natural trends, such as immigration, will certainly in my opinion enable the Church to steward God's manifold grace more effectively.

The information I place before you is to be prayerfully considered with understanding of your stewardship responsibilities as a gifted child of God (see 1 Thess. 5:21; 1 Pet. 4:10). The believers in Berea were commended for their diligence in studying the Word of God. They were seen as *"more fair-minded than those in Thessalonica, in that they received the word with all readiness, and searched the Scriptures daily to find out whether these things were so"* (Acts 17:11). Sometimes believers comfort themselves with the "let me pray about it" and "let me test the spirit" syndrome, where there is neither an intention to pray or to sacrifice busy schedules. Unfortunately, then, satan the accuser of the brethren, knowing the weakness of believers, continues to gain inroads into the Church while we argue over simple matters of prevailing prayer.

However, the time has come for the Church of God to rise up in power *"to root out and to pull down, to destroy and to throw down, to build and to plant"* (Jer. 1:10b). Moreover, Jesus firmly taught, *"Every plant which My heavenly Father has not planted will be uprooted"* (Matt. 15:13).

Endnotes

1. Martin Scott, *Sowing Seeds for Revival* (Tonbridge, Kent: Sovereign World, 2001) p. 22.
2. Larry Lea's contribution in C. Peter Wagner, *Territorial Spirits* (Tonbridge, Kent: Sovereign World, 1991) p. 85.

3. Chuck D. Pierce and Rebecca Wagner Sytsema, *The Future War of the Church* (Ventura, CA: Renew Books, 2001) p. 32.
4. Larry Lea's contribution in C. Peter Wagner, *Territorial Spirits* (Tonbridge, Kent: Sovereign World, 1991) p. 85.
5. Martin Scott, *Sowing Seeds for Revival* (Tonbridge, Kent: Sovereign World, 2001) p. 29.
6. Ibid., p. 35.
7. Larry Lea's contribution in C. Peter Wagner, *Territorial Spirits* (Tonbridge, Kent: Sovereign World, 1991) p. 87.
8. Barbara Wentroble, *A People of Destiny* (Colorado Springs, CO: Wagner Publications, 2000) p. 37.
9. Obii Pax-Harry, *Prophetic Engagement-Issachar Mandate* (Pescara, Italy: Destiny Image Europe, 2006) p. 146.
10. C. Peter Wagner, *Confronting the Powers* (Tonbridge, Kent: Sovereign World, 1996) p. 75.
11. Ibid., p. 75.
12. Martin Scott, *Sowing Seeds for Revival*, republished under the new title, *Gaining Grounds* (Tonbridge, Kent: Sovereign World, 2001) p. 28.
13. Emeka Nwankpa, *Idolatry* (Accra, Ghana: Rehoboth Publishing, 2004) p. 4.
14. C. Peter Wagner, *Territorial Spirits* (Tonbridge, Kent: Sovereign World, 1991) p. 3.

CHAPTER 3

Uncovering Familiar Patterns

I received a rude awakening when the Lord exposed a familiar pattern in the city where my ministry is based. I found I did not have understanding of the ramifications of clear-cut antichrist activities until the light of God shone upon my heart (see Ps. 119:130). It became obvious that our spiritual climate was conducive to evil agendas executed by the enemy using specific channels.

The spirits of death masked as familiar spirits are assigned through familiar spiritual routes and pathways primarily against the Church. As the devil uses familiar patterns (because he lacks originality), unsuspecting targets will suffer numerous spiritual attacks, leading in some cases to hemorrhaging of genuine Kingdom visions. Gradually, demonic assignments attack the hope of believers in Christ—in a city, for instance—and they use the same agenda that Jesus warned of in John 10:10:

> *The thief does not come except to steal, and to kill, and to destroy.*

So, the devil goes all-out to execute the above agenda—to steal, kill, and destroy.

The Bible also teaches us that:

Faith is the substance of things hoped for, the evidence of things not seen (Hebrews 11:1).

Faith substantiates hope; so where there is no hope, faith cannot function. "*Hope deferred makes the heart sick, but when the desire comes, it is a tree of life*" (Prov. 13:12). The devil strikes at the foundation of your faith in order to cause sickness to the heart, and the methods he uses in the spiritual wars of our time are some of the issues I will address in this book. My prayer is that enough people will seek the Lord's face for confirmation, crying out to Him to open the eyes of our understanding (see Eph. 1:17-19). Not every bad piece of news on the news bulletins is a result of natural circumstances; many bear spiritual implications. Satan is intent on achieving his agenda to rob believers of hope. However, the Bible promises believers who are re-created by the blood of Jesus that "*…surely there is a hereafter, and your hope will not be cut off*" (Prov. 23:18). Even a promise such as given in this Scripture may attract spiritual warfare when you make up your mind to appropriate its reality.

UPSETTING THE SPIRITUAL REALMS

Familiar patterns, revealed in the case of our city, worked in a cycle against Kingdom visions and carriers of hope. This established cycle at the time was brought to my attention by my good friend and co-laborer, Judy Duff. She was born in the city I migrated to, so the value of her knowledge was unquantifiable. Our efforts to fulfill divine mandate in our humble ministry were often heavily contended, and I sincerely believe other Kingdom visions were placed under the same demonic siege by the strongman of our city along with his hierarchy of demons. During one telephone conversation, Judy and I plotted cycles of defeat using known information to explain activities in the unseen realm. From then on, my mind was transformed. I seemed to have received supernaturally spiritual gifts that enabled me to excavate unrighteous foundations through prayer. The only way to establish righteous foundations that would hold an enduring work of the holy God is to first excavate unrighteous foundations (see Jer. 1:10). The words of our mouth can carry tremendous power to the point of causing spiritual eruptions (see Mark 11:23-24). By the end of our conversation, Judy and I knew we had upset something in the spiritual realms simply by daring to analyze existing natural patterns that had challenged our spiritual advancement. The enemy's cage had been rattled, and the exposed demon spirits would react by possibly creating difficult circumstances for our ministry.

I later received confirmation of details of our discussion through a dream. The dream I had was of a person whose life provided a *pathway* or access for the spirits that fed on agendas of the spirit of death. Some unknown aspect of the person's life was being revealed as a gateway for demonic activities. The person involved was not only a believer but one who walked in spiritual maturity and boldness. Nothing in this person's demeanour could have prepared anyone's sensory abilities to receive any other information contradictory to their self-professed piety. I was shown the person's legs in the dream, covered from the knees down with strange-looking, dark slugs. I saw many of these creatures crawling up and down, one on top of the other, struggling for space from the knees downward. As I watched, I realized the Lord had given me symbols in my dream for my benefit, to enable me to understand the existing unrighteous foundation of evil within the work of God that had been entrusted into my hands.

The fact that the dark creatures were in motion, moving rapidly up and down the legs, revealed the timing of the message. The Lord was speaking of a present circumstance because the slugs were alive, active, and in motion. The dark slugs were not of any specie known to me, and the fact that the creatures were dissimilar in appearance to the slugs in England where I had the dream suggested they were foreign to the spiritual climate I was residing in. The evil agenda of the slugs originated outside the spiritual climate where I was receiving the revelation, and it was being spiritually imported so that demonic assignments would be completed in the nation where the person who carried them was living—England.

The scene of the dream was also important. Set in the location where I directed the Strategic Prayer School, it indicated the target was that particular house of prayer. The overall message within the dream was to draw my attention to the fact that a person within close spiritual proximity was entrenched in ancestral witchcraft. This fact was represented by the legs covered with vegetation-consuming creatures. So, I had, in effect, finally determined the cause of our struggles, and unfortunately, it was the case of a "household enemy." An in-house demonic assault on the Prayer School was international in commission, imminent in nature, treacherous in choice of carrier, and succeeding at the time in its aim. We were facing a Midianite assignment (see Judg. 6).

PRESSING IN FOR BREAKTHROUGH

I felt a strong urge to contact the person I had seen in my dream, but before I could make a planned telephone call, I found myself interpreting the dream. I later realized that as I did so, I was relying totally on my emotions. I naturally assumed, as most believers would, that the person in question was under some sort of spiritual attack rather than being an attacker. It made sense also to imagine fiery darts of the enemy were being shot from a foreign nation at the person in my dream, but I never considered that the person herself was operating under a Christian disguise. The many slugs I saw fighting for crawling space on her legs clearly represented present standing or positioning in a demonic assignment, which was affecting harvests of seeds of prayer.

I finally rang the person in my dream, who I will refer to as "Mrs. A." In the course of our conversation after sharing details of my dream, I quickly offered an interpretation, one that would keep peace between us. I then suggested a prayer plan that relied on Jeremiah 33:3 as a way forward in seeking to understand the reason for the attack of dark slugs on her legs. Using hindsight, I probably should have picked up on the quiet ease with which the details of my dream and suggested prayer strategy were received at the other end of the telephone line. Mrs. A promised to pray and to telephone her country to confirm whether the slugs I mentioned were common to her nation of birth. Identifying their root would help me identify the root of the demonic assignment coming against me.

A few days later, I received a return telephone call from Mrs. A who confirmed the dark slugs were indeed native to her country of birth. I also remembered noticing in the dream that Mrs. A was not bothered by the presence of such ugly creatures on her legs or by the fact that so many of them were crawling on her legs. Her unperturbed disposition meant that the slugs were a familiar company and her legs were used to carrying them. (Without the anointing, their presence would not have been revealed in our midst—see Isaiah 10:27). Mrs. A informed me with unbelievable confidence about the nature of the slugs.

Interestingly, she said, "They come out at planting time and at harvesting time." Indeed, seasons are confirmed by the Bible: *"To everything there is a season, a time for every purpose under heaven"* (Eccl. 3:1). The Bible also says, *"While the earth remains, seedtime and harvest..."* (Gen. 8:22). The devil understands biblical principles applied to the earth. Therefore, as long as there is an earth, demonic forces will invoke spirits, cast spells, speak curses, make incantations, pour libations, and make sacrifices, all in a bid to generate evil energy with which to harm others.

HARVESTTIME

I received the dream during September 2003, a spiritual and natural harvesting time. The dream revealed both the time of the spiritual attacks against our ministry and the weapon used. Invisible satanic missiles discharged against believers tend to target harvesttimes or times of great expectancy. Such missiles, whether of sickness, unemployment, or any form of bad news, might cause intended harm if bonds of wickedness exist in our lives. The target of the satanic mission of the slugs appeared to be intercessors.

My conclusion led me to believe that much harvest is being aborted in the Body of Christ due to lack of revelation. It seems that when those who have been faithful in prayer are about to receive a reward for their faithfulness, their harvest comes under sabotage.

Again, it would appear the devil was warring against another recognized biblical principle: *"Do not be deceived, God is not mocked; for whatever a man sows, that he will also reap"* (see Gal. 6:7). Now, without interpretation, understanding eludes us; hence, the psalmist called to God for understanding: *"I am Your servant; give me understanding, that I may know Your testimonies"* (Ps. 119:125). We are advised, *"And in all your getting, get understanding"* (Prov. 4:7). There was a process others and I had to go through as *burden bearers* in order to gain experience necessary for our qualification as "witnesses." Part of the end-time call of the prophetic Church will require many to *go through* difficult experiences so that others may pass through into victories.

Our God is Messiah the Breaker:

> *The one who breaks open will come up before them; they will break out, pass through the gate, and go out by it; their king will pass before them, with the Lord at their head* (Micah 2:13).

To speak and to testify for Christ in the endtimes will require much more than head knowledge or repetition of fables.

A SEASON OF WAR

The Holy Spirit revealed that I was shown only the legs and no other body parts as a symbol of the standing or position of the person in question. The legs represented witchcraft that operated in a cycle. Two years later, during another harvest season (September 2005), the spiritual slugs started to manifest. Initially, I struggled with my mind and then with insight that I divinely received regarding the cause of car crashes, job losses, and marriage difficulties experienced by people closest to me. Unlike our brethren of different persuasion, our church folk embraced the Word of God as a weapon with which to war for our lives. With this potent weapon we entered intense spiritual warfare against an obvious onslaught of demonic forces. The Lord opened our spiritual eyes, guiding our church by revelation in a season of war.

In a natural war, such as the Iraqi conflict, opposing armies attack one another during combat. So is the case in spiritual battles. Spiritual warfare for a believer in Jesus Christ called to love, is not against flesh and blood (see 2 Cor. 10:3-4, Eph. 6:12). Our battles are against invisible forces that war against the purposes of God for His children. We are called to love God's creation, but not the devil.

It has been said:

> When a territory has been inhabited by persons who have chosen to offer their worship to demons, the land has been contaminated and those territorial spirits have obtained a right to remain there, keeping the inhabitants captive. It is then necessary to identify the enemy and to go into spiritual battle, until we obtain victory and redeem the territory.[1]

Fundamental to the present-day wars, especially for believers in the Western world, is the fact that the Lord's command to love excludes the devil. We are to hate and resist the works of the devil (see James 4:7). Backlash or counterattacks may occur in spiritual wars, causing casualties as in natural wars. However, regardless of the enemy's reactions, believers are not to abdicate their *stewardship responsibilities* over cities (see Eph. 3:10; 1 Pet. 4:10). Jesus loves cities as is identified and confirmed in the letters to the angels of the seven churches in the Book of Revelation (see Rev. 1:11). The Lord's heart is that none should perish but that all should come to repentance (see 2 Pet. 3:9).

Endnote

1. Caballeros, Harold. *Defeating the Enemy With the Help of Spiritual Mapping*, cited in *Breaking Strongholds in Your City*, C. Peter Wagner (Ventura, CA: Regal Books, 1997) p. 145.

CHAPTER 4

Binding the Strongman

Our Lord Jesus laid down principles for territory-taking, which involves spiritual combat, when He said, "*Or how can one enter a strong man's house and plunder his goods, unless he first binds the strong man? And then he will plunder his house*" (Matt. 12:29). To bind the strongman requires an act of force as we read in Luke 11:21-22:

> *When a strong man, fully armed, guards his own palace, his goods are in peace. But when a stronger than he comes upon him and overcomes him, he takes from him all his armor in which he trusted, and divides his spoils* (Luke11:21-22).

NOT A MATTER OF CHOICE, BUT OF CALLING

The Church has been presented as a weak body, an observation I am not entirely in agreement with. We are simply a people who have not explored all of our options clearly identified in the Word of God. Many believers tend to manipulate understanding of Scriptures to suit their selfish purposes. Adam revealed this trait when he accused Eve, declaring that she was at fault for his personal disobedience. When questioned by God about his obvious rational act of disobedience, he passed the baton of blame and said, *"The woman whom You gave to be with me, she gave me of the tree, and I ate"* (Gen. 1:12b). It is in the fallen man to abdicate responsibility, but not so for those redeemed by the blood of Jesus Christ.

The strongman continues to resist the Church by holding cities, nations, and continents, captive; and there is no other recommended strategy for taking our cities for God but to confront and uproot the strongman. We must follow the example of the early Church who advanced their mission by confronting strongholds in order to establish Kingdom principles and rule in the minds of those they met.

Our call is to share the passion of Jesus (see 2 Pet 3:9) and evangelize the un-evangelized and win back prodigals (see Mark 16:15). Jesus divested all authority to His disciples to accomplish the mission of soul-winning (see Matt. 28:18-19), for He desires that all men be saved (see John 3:16). As a matter of fact, the Lord made clear through His teaching that if you do not share His mission, you are working against Him:

> *He who is not with Me is against Me, and he who does not gather with Me scatters abroad* (Matthew 12:30).

In other words, Jesus Christ made clear that those who do not engage in spiritual warfare to dislodge principalities are *"against Me"* and *"scatters abroad."* The dark forces causing blindness and hardness of hearts in people referred to as *"sons of disobedience"* (see Eph. 2:2) must be disarmed. Thus, spiritual warfare, in my opinion, is not a matter of choice, but of calling. I believe the implications of the words of Jesus Christ in Matthew 12:30 ought to be taken into consideration by the Church, as the Body of Christ accesses her apostolic destiny. Do we wish to gather or scatter abroad?

The apostolic sphere is a warfare, establishing, groundbreaking sphere, necessitating forceful removal of strongholds. The purpose of spiritual warfare is to dislodge demonic principalities that sometimes hold entire cities ransom to sin and idolatry (see Acts 16:16-19). The Church has a responsibility to ensure that places of dwelling on the earth are spiritually safe (see Eph. 3:10), with our foundation firmly built on Christ Jesus, our Chief Cornerstone.

In a bid to understand reasons for the amount of spiritual darkness in the area where I am presently commissioned to and with particular focus on familiar spirits, I began seeking the face of the Lord. Thereafter, the Lord revealed that His children can function in the authority and blessings He died for only if we live holy before our God, which means that all the residing, unrighteous foundations of our lives need to be sorted and weeded out (see 1 Pet. 1:15-16).

FROM GLORY TO GLORY

But we all with unveiled face, beholding as in a mirror the glory of the Lord, are being transformed into the same image from glory to glory, just as by the Spirit of the Lord (2 Corinthians 3:18).

The issue of setting captives free or deliverance should be given more than a casual thought in the Church, especially in the spiritual climates of our time. John was called to a higher level of revelation to hear new things not yet known (see Rev. 4:1). Until I and others had lived through an intense spiritual onslaught during a two-year cycle, I was intolerant of accounts of spiritual warfare and demon possession that I had heard others share. I may have been overly conscious of philosophies I was not spiritually ready for, especially when they were shared with an overbearing force of adamant speakers. However, although I was often suspicious of unfamiliar doctrines, I adopted the practice of the Berean saints who *"received the word with all readiness, and searched the Scriptures daily to find out whether these things were so"* (Acts 17:11b).

Fortunately, the Lord seeks to enlighten our understanding to enable us to redeem the times in an evil day (see Eph. 5:16), and He revealed to me that contending powers now confront the Church from within as "household enemies."

CHAPTER 5

Mind-set for the Days Ahead

The Bible warns extensively of evil days ahead, but the Word says to the believer: *"See that you are not troubled"* (Matt. 24:6b). The troubles of the last days will manifest on the earth, and without accurate interpretation, many people, including believers, will become anxious and uneasy. Therefore, it is important for the Church to understand the purpose for some upheavals that are currently occurring. Hell's fury will seek to challenge the Word of God, but the Bible commands, *"See that you are not troubled."* Trials, tribulations, and even temptations occurring in the life experience of a believer do not happen without our heavenly Father's watchful eyes cast over His children (see 2 Chron. 16:9). Hence, temptations should not overwhelm any person professing Christ (1 Cor. 10:13).

The term *mind-set* depicts a combination of both mind and set. In other words, the mind is already settled on a set of beliefs, and therefore resistant to change. This means it is fixed and rigid. The author John Eckhardt says, "Mind-sets are thought processes of people groups who have developed a way of thinking over centuries of time. ... Mind-sets are not easy to change. ...It takes a strong anointing to break through the defensive barriers in their minds and overcome the pride associated with their way of thinking."[1]

In these last days prophesied in the holy Word of God, believers need not be deceived by satan (see James 4:7). His antics are predicted in the Word of God, so in effect, the devil bears no originality. He operates in cycles, patterns, and sequences in a bid to conceal evil engineered in satanic chambers. The Bible warns us, *"See then that you walk circumspectly, not as fools but as wise, redeeming the time, because the days are evil"* (Eph. 5:15-16). It is important for believers to seek and understand the will of God (see Eph. 1:17-18).

HOLLYWOOD HAS A ROLE IN THE END-TIME WARS

The Lord spoke to me recently to prayerfully watch activities in and around Hollywood, and He revealed that Hollywood would be used extensively to assist the Body of Christ with necessary strategy for the end-time confrontations. He said, *"I will cause the belly of hell to be exposed."* The belly, or in other words, the guts or depth of hell will spew lawlessness, evil, rage, scorn, and wickedness through its mouth using movie-making as a channel. Some of these movies will relate to "wars and rumors of wars" (see Matt. 24:6). My personal assessment of this revelation leads me to believe more horror and violence billed to shock will yet hit our movie screens. Prophetically, such movies are to be received as God's laughter on the enemy: *"He who sits in the Heavens shall laugh; the Lord shall hold them in derision"* (Ps. 2:4). Just as a promise was made to national Israel in Bible days, the Church at present, as spiritual Israel, is also able to receive this covenant promise. So, in effect, the Lord is still laughing at your enemies, who are His enemies.

The command of our Lord Jesus through His holy Word is *"See that you are not troubled."* Many of the difficulties that people will face, in my calculation, will revolve around stewardship of our personal peace. The Lord has not promised a trouble-free lifestyle as a sign of the end of the ages. On the contrary, the words of Matthew 24:6 prepare followers of Christ for victory in a time when there will be much trouble on the earth. The afflictions of a righteous person may be many, but the Lord promises to deliver you from them all (see Ps. 34:19).

RECEIVING THE HEARTBEAT OF HEAVEN

Breaking the Bonds of Wickedness in the Last Days is a preparatory tool for the apostolic missionary who understands the urgency of the hour. The details contained herein may not be of general theological acceptance; however, the emerging spiritual trends reveal new shapes and forms of evil structures. These satanic agendas are shrouded in government policies and outright demonic manifestations in some cases. While evil has been on the earth, even from Adam and Eve's disobedience in the Garden of Eden, such agendas and structures challenging God's ordained purposes should not to be allowed any root.

After the flood in Noah's time, one would have expected that any life on earth flowing out of the only surviving family would have been intelligent enough not to have offended God (see Gen. 6–10). But in Genesis 11, there was an ambitious plan to build a city *"whose top is in the heavens"* (Gen. 11:4b). This endeavor was denied by God who knew the implication of the convergence of consolidated evil. God intervened during this ambitious plot after determining, *"Now nothing that they propose to do will be withheld from them"* (Gen. 11:6b).

The Body of Christ in her stewardship responsibilities must engage the forces seeking to challenge divine purpose for peoples, churches, and lands. God acted in a decisive, proactive manner being God of the universe. He said, *"Come, let Us go down and there confuse their language, that they may not understand one another's speech"* (Gen. 11:7). God "scattered" them abroad, over the face of the earth. The Bible records, *"And they ceased building the city"* (Gen. 11:8b).

God came down as "community" in the Trinity to destroy "false community" activities motivated by anti-God objectives. Our present 21st-century life has inherited problems of past centuries, and has created its own as well, thereby necessitating urgent spiritual response from the Church. A clear problem is once more false demonic communities with an identical antichrist agenda as in the "Babel Coup." These evil communities vigorously drive agendas and efforts geared at overcoming children of the living God, and attempt to wipe out remembrances to our God.

MIND-SET FOR HOLY WAR

Some in the world call for "holy wars," which is simply another phrase for "massacre." But for Christians, our holy war is the war against hopelessness, segregation, selfishness, and self-preservation tendencies of the Western world. Our holy war is war against self harm as we invade the streets with the love of Jesus. However, a believer seeking to engage in the present-day war of the Church must first confront foundational issues in his or her own life. The time has come to examine foundations.

We can be encouraged to know that every war imaginable has been fought and won by Jesus, as you will read through the pages of this book. The victory against invisible forces who war from the mind has been won for would-be believers in Christ Jesus by the Lord's sacrifice of self.

Many Christians erroneously believe in negotiating with the devil regarding issues of deliverance from demonic oppression. Consequently, when faced with an obvious case of demonic oppression or manifestation of demon spirits, if care is not taken, the victim becomes a subject of controversy. Some argue that such a person should be loved and ministered to. Others believe in strenuous regimes as part of a program of deliverance. But the fact is, Christians who open themselves up to demon spirits will be used by such spirits to work against God's own.

Unless believers learn to separate individuals from evil spirits operating through humans, the devil will continue to gain grounds in the Church. The Body of Christ must come into radical holiness to overcome the powers of the endtimes, an important strategy for the endtime wars of the Church. Through several Scriptures, one may deduce that spiritual wars of the endtimes will be fierce, but those who know their God shall be strong and shall carry out exploits (see Dan. 11:32).

CHRISTIAN OR NOT?

Personally, I do not believe a person whose life is yielded to the Lord Jesus Christ in a relationship of love and obedience can be demonized. However, I do believe a Christian whose life is compromised by sin and all manner of unrighteousness can open his or her life up, knowingly or unknowingly, to be used as a channel through which the devil launches his attacks. Such a person may be used to attack destinies or used as a stumbling block to another's purpose, as was the case with Balaam (see Num. 22–24).

For instance, a believer found to be a victim of inherited idolatry or witchcraft, as I will seek to distinguish, has an option of deliverance. The blood of Jesus offers believers continuous access to the throne of God to seek mercy (see Heb. 4:16). Such persons will receive total freedom from inherited or passed-down bondage, if a sincere decision is made to sever links or allegiance to evil deities and covenants. A born-again Christian is a new person in Christ; the old loses value in the new identity inherited in the blood of Jesus. The Bible reminds us of this new status:

> *Therefore, if anyone is in Christ, he is a new creation; old things have passed away; behold, all things have become new* (2 Corinthians 5:17).

When dealing with such a believer, the first suggested step for a leader in spiritual authority over his or her life would be to separate the individual from the invading spirits. The Bible equates rebellion to the sin of witchcraft, in which case pastoral response should be focused on ministry leading to confession of sins to God.

However, ancestral witchcraft bonds individuals to the initiating deity, and to undo effects of ancestral witchcraft would require absolute cooperation of the victim of witchcraft as you will read in subsequent chapters. Bondage to ancestral spirits whether of clear-cut initiated witchcraft or worship of water gods, is a serious matter. The Western mind-set understands much about the Jezebel, Absalom, Haman, or Leviathan spirits. However, with global paradigms and trends as they stand, the Church needs to expand her knowledge of the enemies we are to evict from illegal occupation.

STEWARDS ARE GOVERNORS

The primary pursuit of the Body of Christ is to worship the Lord in spirit and truth (see John 4:23-24), as we are entrusted with stewardship of the earth and of the heavens (see Matt. 28:18-19; Mark 16:15).

To the intent that now the manifold wisdom of God might be made known by the church to the principalities and powers in the heavenly places (Ephesians 3:10).

Spiritual warfare is not a matter of choice for apostolic agents, but of calling. Each person has been given a gift to minister in-house as *"good stewards of the manifold grace of God"* (1 Pet. 4:10b). As disciples of the same grace, we are now to dislodge demonic powers that cause spiritual blindness and hardness of hearts. However, to engage in strategic level spiritual warfare and to dislodge the said evil forces, we need to prepare against spiritual land mines and other compromising issues. Remember the devil is the "accuser of the brethren" (see Rev. 12:10).

Endnote

1. John Eckhardt, *Moving in the Apostolic* (Ventura, CA: Renew Books, 1999) p. 59.

CHAPTER 6

Breaking the Two-Year Cycle

I was commissioned to an area within our city known for witchcraft, freemasonry, new age, and satanism. As a matter of fact, when I mentioned the name of the area given to me by the Lord, my experienced pastor replied, "That has to be the Lord." I honestly believe the Lord saved me from analyzing the implication of that statement even as doors closed to natural enquiries I made, including contacting some assemblies. The human side of me desired information from experienced intercessors, pastors, and prophets about the area called Moseley in Birmingham, England. But the Spirit of the Lord spoke repeatedly, "The foundation will take three years, so keep building your foundation."

An important part of our foundation work would involve rooting out evil that would seek to lay itself out like a python. The Greek word for "witchcraft" is *python*. A python is a large constrictor. Constrictors kill their prey by slowly squeezing the breath out of them. John Eckhardt believes python spirits attempt to squeeze the life out of the Church by stopping the flow of the Holy Spirit.[1] Unless those called to establish a new work follow the pattern of Heaven, the serpent will crawl into the foundations to destroy new plants of the Lord. The enemy will use situations, circumstances, and even persons to demolish divine plans; and he attacks strengths and weaknesses that are not submitted to the Almighty God. Yet Jesus is the Chief cornerstone of any church that would stand (see Eph. 2:20). The Church is to be *"the pillar and ground of the truth"* (1 Tim. 3:15b).

Eighteen months after planting Resurrection Life Assembly, the Lord spoke clearly to me, "Prepare to break the two-year cycle." Before then, the Lord warned the leadership of our church to lay low and not to advertise ourselves across the city for three years. With the benefit of hindsight, our hearts now rejoice at God's wisdom.

We discovered that a major part of the foundation stage involved destroying an established spiritual pathway through which a strange attack would "scatter" congregations by first attacking the pastor (see Zech. 13:7). At the end of the second year, the intended targets of these foul principalities would either change ministry identity, leadership, or lose life of the vision.

Demonic agents often operate in predetermined sequences and patterns, so in order to disrupt and destroy their activities, the sequence of attack needed to be discerned. While battling for our safety, several dreams and other revelation, given not only to myself but to others as well over three years, started to fit together throughout my ordeal. I was comforted to know that the Lord was with me throughout my ordeal. The same spirit, ravaging spiritual harvests, found its way into our church. I was warned repeatedly to "beware of the two-year cycle." But I tried to rationalize and dismiss obvious signs that if I had heeded, could have saved much suffering.

CLOSING GAPS

My efforts to understand a pattern, as I tarried in prevailing prayer, yielded much fruit. However, I kept losing spiritual momentum almost as soon as I gained some strength. In sharing my revelations with whom

I thought to be the safety of church leadership, I lost ground. Mrs. A was still bonded in a cord of wickedness to ancestral spirits and had not yet been exposed. Electrical equipment broke down within weeks while our recording equipment mocked us with blank Cds after services. My natural casualness on a serious matter cost me dearly. At a point, we realized that a reinforcement of evil armies had been dispatched as spates of car crashes started to reoccur. Our prayers seemed to have been weakened, and the Lord revealed a need to rise in greater authority than the evil forces we were seeking to evict. We then incorporated stringent fasting regimes with the Word of God in our mouths.

By September in the two-year cycle, from the time our church was planted, the aggression of the enemy had become too intense to ignore. Suddenly, meaningless car accidents, challenges to marriages, job losses, and financial dryness began to occur in a clear and visible pattern. Every visitor who returned was subsequently targeted. My attention was especially captured by five different car crashes involving the rear side of cars belonging to members of our congregation. *Why not any other side of cars and why only the rear?* I wondered. As a pastor, I was at that point in time, unable to ascertain the source of obvious spiritual bombardment we were under. However, I felt that the intensity and detailed manner with which demonic missiles were being launched indicated the presence of an in-house agent. In cases of ancestral witchcraft, incessant attacks that appear successful usually indicate the presence of an in-house enemy. A person of your own household is armed with your weaknesses, and any arrows shot from close proximity are more likely to hit the intended target. The enemy was constantly striking in many disguises; and on the day he was finally exposed, he appeared as an old person.

ENDNOTE

1. John Eckhardt, *Moving in the Apostolic* (Ventura, CA: Renew Books, 1999) p. 132.

CHAPTER 7

Unmasking Demonic Agents

THE PAST IS KEY TO THE FUTURE

The fact that I could identify the natural identities of the demonic agents attacking our destinies as I described earlier was a real bonus. An enemy from the past had tracked my life up until a new beginning for me—pastoring, and to defeat this enemy would mean going back into the past for understanding that would unlock my future.

Another advantage I enjoyed was from a previous experience gained 12 years earlier. During that time, I had to battle for the life of my young son from a caregiver who was involved in ancestral witchcraft activities. My mother and I had agreed to set a prayer watch with fasting as a weapon in the month of March 1993. We needed to understand strange activities around our environment that had been dismissed for two years. I will never forget the day things came to a head in our home. It began with family prayers. The Lord drew my attention to the fact that my son's caregiver was not in the prayer circle nor was she linking hands with any of us. The Bible teaches, *"Can two walk together, unless they are agreed?"* (Amos 3:3). It is important to watch actions, reactions, and even speech of people, whether Christian or not.

Later that night, I was surprised to see her walking into my bedroom. The picture was so clear that I believed I was in a natural experience and asked her what she wanted. As I walked towards her at my bedroom door, I was shocked because all I saw was a thick black cloud, and out of that cloud came an invisible hand that hit my neck. This all happened in a revelatory dream after family prayers.

Later, I was in so much pain that I needed a doctor's appointment and medical treatment for a sore throat. My throat throbbed for two weeks while Mom and I prayed with faith for strategy to get the caregiver set free from the apparent oppression. Fortunately, we surrounded ourselves with teachings from great men of faith such as Kenneth Hagin, Kenneth Copeland, and Jerry Savelle.

Four months later, I encountered another agent of ancestral witchcraft, not in England, but in a different country this time. The young man in question worked for a family I was visiting in Nigeria. In this second experience, I watched as the man casually strolled into the living room (in the spirit) of my host family at around 2:00 a.m. Again the scene before me was so real that I thought it was happening in the natural. I casually called out his name, asking why he was back in the house so late. Instead of an answer, I was punched about in the spirit. I started fighting back. The Lord had prepared me for this encounter through a book I had stayed up that night to read. The book was written by a confessed warlock who had become an active evangelist for the Gospel of Jesus. My English trained mind could not comprehend all the things I read in the book. He wrote about nighttime astral travels to harm people, initiation into witchcraft by food, and all manner of strange activities he and his fellow warlocks had conducted against the Body of Christ. The man wrote that he was so high up in demonic hierarchy that he was the fourth person to satan. I believe that when referring to satan, he was referring to the strongman over that nation.

The scene in my living room was happening not long after reading about the former warlock's surrender to Jesus while on assignment to disrupt a crusade in the eastern parts of Nigeria. He wrote of how many of his army died just as the name Jesus was mentioned by the crusade speaker. By this, I believe the spirits of his fellow astral travellers were crushed and probably returned to their bedrooms in the natural.

Apparently, every time the name and blood of Jesus was mentioned, he lost more soldiers until he found himself standing alone amidst a crowd of passionate worshippers. He was arrested by the Holy Spirit when the speaker spoke by a word of knowledge that the crusade had been visited by a warlock and then commanded the warlock to come to the platform in Jesus' name.

So, I was reading the testimony of the warlock who had become a mighty warrior for the Lord when Mr. A. strolled into my friend's home at 2:00 a.m., in the spirit. I was watching him in an open vision (supernatural experience). He was evidently a strongman over their home, being meticulous and efficient in the natural, which had won him the trust of his employers. Note that agents of ancestral witchcraft often possess a strong natural trait of unusual organizational skills that attract dependency from their victims. Unfortunately, when they attack, usually after midnight, their victims are very often those closest and dearest to them.

TESTED IN THE FURNACE OF AFFLICTIONS

Behold, I have refined you, but not as silver; I have tested you in the furnace of affliction" (Isaiah 48:10).

Ten years after confronting the first case of ancestral witchcraft, the Lord began a process that would bring me face-to-face with another agent. I was being prepared to unmask a major coalition of evil with a strong European and African spiritual partnership. My challenges of the past were now weapons needed to execute the judgment of God on the devil. I was also reminded of several confrontations with witch doctors and other principalities on a mission trip in 2003 to the southern region of Africa, which was notorious for witchcraft.

In the case of severe witchcraft as our congregation faced, the most important key to overcoming the negative force is exposure. The Lord clearly said to me, "You cannot defeat an enemy you cannot identify." I interpreted the Lord's words as a call to prayer.

CHAPTER 8

Breaking Familiar Patterns

CONFRONTING EVIL

Jesus Christ gallantly defeated satan and his cohorts with His precious blood. The victory report of this epic battle is timeless with continual blessings for those who would dare to appropriate its benefit. As saints battling the present-day spiritual wars of the Church, we need to remember that righteousness is as crucial to effectiveness in ministry in the last days as it was in the beginning. The devil is manifesting in all manner of disguises, infiltrating so-called Spirit-filled meetings undetected. I sincerely believe that I and others were afforded the personal privilege to endure and defeat a demonic coalition that placed our lives under siege so that our experiences might be shared far and wide.

An important emerging spiritual trend of evil is the coalition of demonic activities converging across the globe. Evil attracts evil; thus, alliances are formed across nations, adding flavor to existing forms of occultism and strengthening antichrist agendas. Migration trends and immigration routes are key avenues for some dimensions of evil that require attention of the Church.

In Genesis, when Rachel stole the family idols and carried them with her as they travelled, her father, Laban, pursued Jacob and his household with the intent of recovering them (see Gen. 31:19-35). According to the ancient law in the area of Haran, the eldest son of a family held the honor of inheriting the family idols. Although Rachel's intentions are not made clear in this Bible narrative, one might assume that she desired a link or attachment to her native religion. Rachel's case points to the importance that can be placed on family idols, and more significantly, the fact that idolatry can be given "legs" with which to operate in new spiritual territories.

Just as Christians search for churches when they migrate to another nation of their choice, so is the case for occultism practitioners who naturally seek others attracted to their same dark ways. The experiences I have attempted to communicate point to the globalization of evil. Freemasons locate lodges wherever they reside unless the choice to disengage from the fraternities is consciously made. Born-again, Spirit-filled Christians possess intrinsic supernatural abilities to unravel mysteries of the dark regardless of their origin. Hence, the devil instigates segregation, racism, nepotism, favoritism and much more, to establish and maintain dividing walls. Beyond multiculturalism is true unity, a most important prerequisite to the dunamis of God, necessary to unmask strange spirits now in our midst. Our congregation was not only a cross-racial congregation, but the Spirit of God made us "one" after a two-year journey, during which we were exposed to the devil's ploys by our carnal ways.

OBEDIENCE IS KEY

On the fateful night that the real source of untold woes, including threats to human lives, destabilizing of family life and worse, "was revealed," I simply changed a familiar routine of my husband's and mine. I asked to change sleeping positions with my husband purely by inspiration of the Holy Spirit. Surprisingly, my rational husband yielded to what would in the past have been seen as a whole load of rubbish or the effects of too many late nights. No sooner had I lain down on my husband's side of the bed than an old lady appeared before me (in the spirit). I was shocked, confused, and not sure what to do.

Seconds before, I had barely considered unusual sounds coming from my bathroom window, directly facing my borrowed sleeping position. I was still pondering over what I thought was an illusion—an image of a person breezing in like air through the window—when the old woman suddenly stood before me on my husband's side of the bed. I heard my spirit call out, "I know who you are," and I named the person, once more by divine inspiration, which was a young woman who I knew in the natural. As soon as I spoke the name, the young woman seemed to jump out of the body of the old woman. My loud gasp woke up my husband and informed my mind I was still in a supernatural spiritual experience. With benefit of hindsight, I can confidently relate this experience as real life due to the clarity and reality of my encounter with a demonic agent. Yet at the same time, I was in a dream. As I named the lady, I began to feel the weight of punches on my body. Again, it felt like I was going through a natural experience. I then responded first with punches, my hands flying in the air, with my husband leaping up several times to my flying hands and asking, "Are you all right?" Inspired by the Holy Spirit, I began declaring Scriptures that reminded the devil of his predetermined woeful failure and defeat (see Col. 2:14-15). I was amazed to watch as the Scriptures I spoke aloud hit her like fist punches of a heavyweight boxer. Her reactions and apparent weakness as I spoke the Scriptures gave me the confidence to continue to speak aloud every known Scripture the Holy Spirit illuminated before me.

The battle with the old lady, who became a young woman known to me, continued until about 3:00 a.m. I then looked at my bedside clock and wondered why she seemed to disappear. I did not realize at that time that the devil's watch ended at 3:00 a.m.; and the dread of demonic agents is the Lord's watch, which begins at 3:00 a.m., at which time those that derive occultism powers to astral travel dash back to their physical bodies. I spoke Scriptures until at least 6:00

a.m. I was so shocked by my experience, half wishing I had been in a bad dream, and then rang my assistant. I related my experience to her as a "spiritual attack" and a case of "stolen identity" with which the devil sought to accuse the young woman who was in my bedroom a few hours previously.

The Holy Spirit, my Friend and Teacher, once more inspired me to ask my assistant to telephone the lady's workplace in order to discern her state of mind. Unsure of the traumatizing experience I had endured, I shared the fact that my mother often taught me that demonic agents who astral travel to attack sleeping victims often manifest physical signs of an injury they sustain should their victims respond. I knew I responded and possibly overreacted, having named a considerable amount of Scriptures, which in my late mother's estimation should have left the demonic agent ill for at least a few days. To our shock, her workplace said she had rung in sick when the office opened up that morning. My assistant and I knew we were on to something beyond our comprehension. We felt it necessary to work with time and telephone her home to discern her physical and mental state. We were finally convinced of our worst fear when she responded that she had suddenly fallen ill. But with familiar Christian language, she intended to throw us off track by telling my assistant that she needed to "seek the face of the Lord" through the day.

From experience, I knew a spiritual battle of a different magnitude had begun, since I, as her pastor, was now aware of her nighttime job. I sought counsel from pastors within the western world where the events were unfolding and those of the continent where the ancestral spirits and covenants were being invoked. My next line of action was to place leaders in our church on the third watch (12:00 a.m. to 3:00 a.m.), praying with the first few prayers in the prayer section of this book. We embraced the blood of Jesus, the blood of sprinkling, as our weapon, and placed our trust in God. Most of us had nothing to lose, having suffered physical and spiritual harassment for nearly two years. Following counsel of demonologists, I confronted the lady, who had significant responsibilities in our church, before the leaders.

Today, we all wish it had been a bad dream. After engaging four pastors during a three-month period to assist with her deliverance, unfortunately, she died in a fatal crash not having received deliverance from bonds of ancestral wickedness. I realized I had heard accurately when the Lord informed me she would reject deliverance. Such is the fate of men and women bound to ancestral witchcraft and idol worshipping, many sitting in churches, willing to serve the Lord but caught in allegiance to family idols.

To unmask these demonic agents requires a radical, righteous-in-Christ, praying body of believers. These are the agents that are sometimes behind our swelling numbers that make up our mega-churches where detection is all the more difficult, except by radical holiness. The time has come to account for our human resources. The question is the same as Joshua asked the "Man" who stood opposite him by Jericho—"Are you for us or for our adversaries?"(Josh. 5:13b).

CHAPTER 9

Setting the Captives Free

Jesus Christ declared at the beginning of His ministry, having been baptized by the Holy Spirit:

The Spirit of the Lord is upon Me, because He has anointed Me...to set at liberty those who are oppressed (Luke 4:18).

The practical works of Jesus Christ documented in the Gospels attest to this pronouncement He made in Nazareth. In Isaiah 61:1-2, the deliverance of Israel from exile in Babylon is prophesied and repeated in the words of Luke 4:18-19. Fulfillment of Isaiah 61 came during the messianic age with the Messiah Himself. Jesus' birth, ministry, and death unfolded, expressed, and extended the Kingdom of God. Jesus transferred responsibility to His disciples "and gave them power and authority over all demons, and to cure diseases. He sent them to preach the kingdom of God and to heal the sick" (Luke 9:1-2).

The Church of the present age bears responsibility to preach the message of the cross which remains foolishness to those who are perishing (see 1 Cor. 1:18). Preaching with the accompanying power rather than enticing words of human wisdom will cause the Kingdom of God to advance in believers presently (see 1 Cor. 2:4-5; 4:20). Churches professing Christ can no longer afford to be motivated by ephemeral, passing fancies that do not guarantee Heaven or effect change on the earth. Birth pangs of the apostolic Church over the years have been felt in the various "shakings" translated in sufferings, tribulations, and so forth. Reality of the age of the present Church is my motivation for writing this book.

Years of ignorance of strategic level spiritual warfare did not earn me condemnation but instead prepared me as a humble student of the Holy Spirit. Presence of ancestral idolatry, witchcraft, occultism within four walls of church buildings, and I dare say in some cases, leadership of ministries, is a shocking reality many believers need to come to terms with. I do not advocate a witch hunt, but strongly encourage spiritual awareness and positioning in Christ that makes practice of evil impossible amongst Spirit-filled congregations. The devil has infiltrated Christian gatherings, warming its way into hearts of even prophetic leaders. Present-day evil, typical of pythons, appears to strangle churches, eventually putting out the fire of passion and leaving in its place apathetic numbers incapable of four hours of consistent prayers in most cases. Indeed, my church received a rude awakening to new levels of occultism in our foundation years.

An enduring work of the Lord must be built on a solid foundation with Jesus Christ as the Chief Cornerstone (see Eph. 2:20-22). Numbers should no longer be made the focal point of churches but the equipping of the numbers, the saints, to rule and reign in the love and power of Jesus.

The apostolic mandate of churches will bring us into a face-off and direct confrontation with the enemy. We found in our experience, that the anointing, and only the true anointing of God, exposes the enemy within. Not one aspect of our familiar patterns, routines, programs is a threat to the enemy within who might also be a part of the congregation. In terms of human efforts, we saw folly in attempting to placate or preach to a demon spirit possessing the physical body of any persons, but instead, we, through prayer, aggressively demanded eviction of such a spirit. Personally, I lost time and momentum when my westernized mind doubted obvious signs of demonic activities around me. The Holy Spirit, our universal Spirit of truth, taught and inspired the prayers with which I was able to lead my congregants out of the valley of the shadow of death.

The Church is to battle for the souls of persons bonded to wickedness, but to do that, believers need to search their lives for residing evil. It is important to bear in mind that our spiritual wars are not against flesh and blood, so we cannot war with man-made weapons. The devil is a deceiver who needs human vessels to transmit his evil so he recruits compromised hearts of even believers (see Rom. 6:23). We must heed the Bible's warning not to be carnally minded, for the mind of the flesh leads to death (see Rom. 8:6).

ANCESTRAL AND SPIRITUAL WITCHCRAFT

The Lord removed His hedge of protection from Saul as king over Israel because of disobedience which was qualified as rebellion, akin to witchcraft. Because disobedience to the divine will of God is classified as rebellion, and rebellion, witchcraft, one might safely assume that any person not yielded to the will of God opens his or her heart to spiritual witchcraft. On the other hand, ancestral witchcraft involves initiation of the soul of a person, bonding his or her heart to idols, deities, or any source of power receiving their homage.

The initiation rites usually involve shedding of blood to ratify demonic agreements made with deities, idols, cults, and so forth. In some cases, family lines are chosen as a mark of respect as a gateway to the deities worshipped by entire communities. Initiation of bloodlines often comes with far-reaching consequences, transferred down through generations. Call to duty for persons bonded to evil, such as ancestral witchcraft, is by invocation, as opposed to anointing for a commissioned disciple of Christ. Disciples of Christ are ordained by presbyteries, sometimes by laying on of hands, or even prophesying (see 1 Tim. 4:14; 2 Tim. 1:6). But persons bonded to evil are located in the spirit realm by witch doctors, caretakers of shrines, priestesses, and other gatekeepers of evil, using omens, tokens, and even talking drums. When the lot falls upon such persons to serve their deities, they will unfortunately be located in the spirit if their hearts are not fully yielded to the Lord after deliverance upon becoming born again. Similar to electronics, they respond to remote controlled signals of their fraternities, boldly attacking those that stand in their way—believers in Christ Jesus.

Persons who are bonded to ancestral spirits and who also observe rites of deities normally move around in locations where the spirits they worship maintain contact. They bear allegiance to demonic covenants made on their behalf by family members or themselves. Environments are not solely responsible for influences that change personalities for good or bad. True change must emanate from inside of a person. Similar to Rachel, many people still migrate across the globe with previous allegiances to ancestral spirits. These spirits, as familiar spirits, track lives of their subjects, challenging their newfound life in Christ. People movement is not the idea of national governments but of commission to those that would serve the Lord Jesus (see Mark 16:15-20; Matt. 28:18-20).

My congregation and I have encountered spirits at work against multiplication of Kingdom vision. Church planting is the devil's nightmare, so he seduces congregations to swell into huge masses rather than multiply into 120 world changers. The time has come to flush out evil from amidst well-meaning worshippers. Apostolic prayer and prophetic lifestyle are important for the journey ahead. To those who do the will of God, He promises "Lo, I am with you always, even to the end of the age" (Matt. 28:20b).

Prayer Shield

Introduction

In order to effectively apply the principles in this book, it is important to bear in mind that your spiritual wars are not against humans, but against spirit beings in the invisible realm. I have found it necessary to include a prayer shield section to support some perspectives highlighted in previous chapters.

MOVING TO THE NEXT LEVEL

My prayer language was radically enhanced by the Holy Spirit as I battled day and night to maintain peace in my borders during 2005. I was privileged to serve in a Strategic Prayer School initiative in partnership with pioneers, Rod and Julie Anderson, of Prayer For The Nation, U.K. Through facilitating, teaching, training, and engaging in the art of intercession, I was also privileged to serve many destinies. However, nothing prepared me for the force of spiritual warfare, for which I attained a level necessary to do battle at the time.

Often, believers speak of a "moving to the next level" experience with an attitude that suggests we actually have a choice as to how, when, and where the next level is. But now, with hindsight, I can confidently caution those who suppose that a next-level experience comes without contention. On the contrary, contentions intensify according to whatever level the Lord is taking you to. Amazingly, the Lord does not give a full picture of incidents occurring in the process of maturity, some of which I would have opted out of. Our expectations of "next-level" arrival need to be evaluated with serious thought given to how we get to the next destination in God. In my case, I advanced through many tribulations, just as the early Church testified of. A whole new world of experience opened up to me with the Holy Spirit firmly by my side, teaching me how I must pray.

These are the same prayers I now share with you throughout the next several sections. These are only suggested guidelines, and not absolutes to be substituted for the Holy Spirit's voice and direction.

REVELATION FROM THE HOLY SPIRIT

My aim in writing is to encourage those who would be prepared and do battle as end-time soldiers of Christ in the last day. Spiritual battles against believers are intensifying on a daily basis, and inviting the Lord to fight on your behalf will require you to break every bond of wickedness in your life that has empowered the enemy against you.

The Kingdom of God can only be advanced by revelation (see Hos. 4:6; Isa. 5:13). I had been quite naïve about spiritual warfare and intolerant of stories of ceaseless deliverance meetings until I and other people I know experienced those things for ourselves. Then I began to enter new territory as a pastor. I had been in itinerant ministry for several years before the Lord spoke to me and said, "Build Me an ark." After several meetings with my then pastor, the time to move finally arrived. I remember my pastor saying, "Moseley, that has to be God." Not being native to Birmingham, I could only rely on the Holy Spirit's revelation of strongholds in an area that was fast becoming a modern hub for occultist activities.

Introduction

TRANSPARENCY AND HOLINESS

I still do not believe in ascribing every problem to the devil, nor should you. Moreover, so often we inadvertently wish away experiences that are for our benefit in learning. I now believe the Lord allows certain events to occur so that His children are able to step back and seek understanding. Some have said experience is the best teacher, a perspective I have found bears witness with me. An unprepared soldier is an easy target in a battlefield. Sin leaves us unprepared, marring a believer's life, as does *"every weight…which so easily ensnare us…"* (Heb. 12:1b).

At times in the past, the Body of Christ has fought with a defeatist mentality—some attempting to fight in Saul's armor (see 1 Sam. 17:38-39). But weapons of the past may not suffice in a modern war. To fight in the spiritual wars of today, it is important that you sever any links to sin, including family line bondages. My church and I knew the only way we could break the pattern of near-death experiences was to rise to a new level of holiness. Our first covenant with one another was of transparency. The more open people were with their lives, the closer we were to exposing the enemy within us. While satan practices a habit of isolation before extinction, we were led by the Holy Spirit to practice the opposite, which is transparency.

TO SPEAK IN TONGUES, OR NOT

The second strategy I had to take responsibility for as a pastor was to ask for all prayers to be said in understanding—in our case, the English language, and not in tongues (see 1 Cor. 14:5-11). The Holy Spirit had revealed that there was a presence of a perverted language spoken as "tongues" in the midst of our worship. Consequently, I could have come under attack of religious spirits who believe tongues should be spoken publicly regardless of interpretation.

At times, our religious minds forbid us to question or imagine that these "tongues" can actually be inspired by sources other than the Holy Spirit. Every member of a church assumes that once in the building, all aspects of worship flow from Heaven, as did the members of my congregation and I until the Lord led us to question unnecessary spiritual warfare around us. Only then did we realize our church had been invaded by something unfamiliar. However, I knew the Lord was with us, as we were in the area that He had initially sent us into. As an assembly, we had been sent with an apostolic commission but were operating with a church mind-set. Our awakening, which began with a two-page prayer guide, is in your hands today as a book.

When addressing the issue of spiritual gifts in the church at Corinth, the apostle Paul said, *"But now, brethren, if I come to you speaking with tongues, what shall I profit you unless I speak to you either by revelation, by knowledge, by prophesying, or by teaching?"* (1 Cor. 14:6). The Scripture is clear on this important gift.

THE POWER OF "AMEN"

I listened to the voice of the Lord and followed every step as the Holy Spirit directed me. Uppermost in my thoughts was protection of the lives given me to serve and lead. As I obeyed the Lord and encouraged praying in a known language, it became obvious that we had a group in leadership positions within our church who never said, "Amen." Not using "Amen," which means "Let it be so," was an indication of an agenda to disestablish any prayer we made.

Yet when that group of people led prayer meetings, as the custom of the church required, everyone present established with an "Amen" to whatever they spoke as "tongues." I do not mean to portray that I was experienced or knowledgeable on a matter that I was just as ignorant of as anyone else. I'm simply stating that such is the reality of the present-day war of the Church.

A few months before, so much of the enemy's plans were revealed by the mercies of the Lord, and I was inspired by the Lord to teach our congregation the meaning and significance of "Amen." So many things began to make sense, and events that inspired this book began to unfold. Our leadership was at a point in time armed with so much revelation of the root cause of senseless spiritual attacks that the enemy stood no chance. I was confident in the Lord's ability to war on our behalf because we were obedient in observing

Introduction

instructions received for our foundation years. For example, the Lord had instructed me not to print brochures or take out advertisements about our church as a new church in town. I was simply commanded to "lay low" for three years; repeatedly, the Holy Spirit warned that our foundation would take three years to build. This book is coming to you after three years and an encounter with some of satan's best soldiers, but in every contention the blood of Jesus proved too much for satan and his cohorts. I often remind those, whom I have had the privilege to serve as leader, an important truth—the devil attacks you with what he knows you ought to understand, and not by issues you have chosen not to understand.

May the Lord bless you as you pray. Amen.

PRAYER SECTION I

Spiritual War

IDENTIFY THE ENEMY

Past compromises can affect present and future obedience. The Bible cautions, *"Therefore submit to God. Resist the devil and he will flee from you"* (James 4:7).

Bondage is defined as "involuntary servitude and slavery." Quin Sherrer and Ruthanne Garlock believe "someone who is in bondage is: dominated, restrained, usually by compulsion, subjugated to a controlling person or force."[1] A person who gives room to sin or curses that control their life, in line with the definition above, is one living in involuntary servitude and slavery. A slave is bound to his or her master. Why do so many believers experience meaningless trials and encounter challenges with alarming frequency? How does a believer endowed with so many benefits emanating from the sacrifice of the life of Jesus endure countless spiritual warfare? Indeed, many Christians seem to be losing ground. These and many other issues dominated my thought process during a two-year period of intense training for future apostolic responsibilities.

Closing Racial Gaps

The Church's impact on many cities, especially in western societies, has been abysmal, if the truth were to be told. We have seemed to rotate ideas and recycle experiences in a bid to remain relevant in a world we have been commissioned to impact. I have come to believe, in the light of experiences giving rise to this book, that a major part of satan's agenda is to initiate culture pollution in some congregations. However, churches are to embrace God's *manifold wisdom* expressed through various cultures represented in their congregation. Every race is an expression of God's multifaceted wisdom (see Eph. 3:10). Conversely, satanic agendas mimic preordained plans of God to pervert the same. Culture can be used to corrupt God's purposes, yet the Bible advocates resistance to the *"scepter of wickedness"* (Ps. 125:3a). The devil is the same, even while he dresses in different costumes of nations, so dependence on perspectives from one culture may becloud views from unfamiliar cultures.

Satanic agendas remain the same, although they may be expressed at times in the familiarity of various national dynamics, such as language, mannerism, and dress code. Quin Sherrer and Ruthanne Garlock express an opinion that lends support to the message I seek to communicate. They say, "Each of us come to Christ from different backgrounds and cultures, and at varying levels of maturity."[2] So, each believer carries cultural bondages and advantages able to create the synergy lacking in some spiritual warfare initiatives. Therefore, it is important to marshal every troop in the Lord's war so that insight can be gained into God's hidden riches in men (see 2 Cor. 4:7). Satan often attacks to destroy attributes you never thought were part of you, else he would not have thought it was worth launching an attack in the first place.

The Bible makes clear that partial knowledge is a fact—a humbling reality, so we need every tribe and every tongue worshipping together. We know only in part and prophesy in part (see 1 Cor. 13:9). My balanced experience and multicultural mind-set saved my life at a time when I could have adopted a western mind-set or allowed for flexibility of the eastern experience. For instance, a dream of a demonic assignment may be revealed to an intercessor in the West through the familiar picture of a burger-eating demon. Another part of the same revelation may be received by another intercessor in Africa of the same demon eating a maize meal. We need a specialized anointing on people within the Body of Christ who are able to understand the common language of Heaven, albeit expressed in different continents. The fact of the matter is that the world now lies on a hard drive of a home computer.

A Global Community Emerging

To engage in strategic level warfare, present-day believers need to break bonds of wickedness and every demonic covenant in their own lives. This is absolutely vital if we are to utilize higher levels of spiritual sight necessary to defeat some unusual satanic formations of our day (see Rev. 4:1). The earth can be seen only through the eyes of Jesus Christ (see Ps. 24:a; 2 Chron. 16:9).

The Church needs to operate strategic bodies, similar to the United Nations, that are responsible for receiving and examining spiritual espionage, similar to the sort I have shared. Efficient dissemination of tested revelation necessary for apostolic warfare will be helpful to a wider body of intercessors who can learn from the experiences of others. Information received from apostles and prophets will assist intercessors and enable them to pray accurately and more effectively. While we are to be thankful for apostles who have pioneered in this area, we also need more strategists for the present-day spiritual wars. With Islam and some new age movements presenting threats to the advancing of the Kingdom of God in some nations and continents, more information on strategic level spiritual warfare needs to be commonly available to intercessors in such nations. Although I believe I am stating an obvious fact, it is necessary in some instances to emphasize "the obvious" in order to draw attention to *fresh insight* overlooked, because the obvious at times becomes too obvious, leading to apathy.

Counterattacks and back lashes are unfortunate realities in apostolic spheres and stratospheres. So, do not be put off or allow fear to interfere with your prayers. Several other believers and I have engaged the prayers in this book, experiencing instant results in some cases. It is not unusual to have revelatory experiences with the Lord opening the heavens over your life so that you can see *"unsearchable truths"* as you pray (see Jer. 33:3). Revelation ushers in understanding and lessens casualties in the spiritual wars of the present day.

Your purpose in praying ought not to center on ways of escaping from difficulties. Rather, you should concentrate efforts in partnering with Heaven to discover new levels of apostolic authority with which to advance the Kingdom of God. Born-again, Spirit-filled Christians referred to as "believers" will suffer afflictions (see Isa. 48:10). As a matter of fact, the early Church expressed an opinion I am finding to be true in my personal walk with Christ. They said, *"We must through many tribulations enter the kingdom of God"* (Acts 14:22b). While you are not to covet afflictions, it is important to see them as stepping-stones to the future. Remember to focus your attention and channel your energies in prayer to deal with unrighteous foundations in your life or family line. An important function of our corporate mantle as the Body of Christ requires every believer to prophetically engage with God's seasons and times. A good example for us to follow is the tribe of Issachar who were honored for fulfilling their stewardship responsibilities to Israel (see 1 Chron. 12:32).

Divine Calling

I sincerely believe every true believer in Christ Jesus is positioned in cities and nations by the Lord according to Acts 17:26: *"And He has made from one blood every nation of men to dwell on all the face of the earth, and has determined **their preappointed times and the boundaries of their dwellings**"* (emphasis added).

An integral part of residence requires some level of responsibility to the land or area, which includes honoring laws and regulations. Every inch of land on planet earth belongs to your God who has placed you in your city at this present time as His representative. The devil understands the divine nature, so he strives to discourage you from fulfilling your God-ordained destiny. Moreover, dealing with root causes of problems without seeking to understand the spiritual climate harboring them may not yield lasting solutions. If you think about it, certain climates are kinder to some natural dispositions. For example, countries with warm weather are often attractive to elderly people. Likewise, spiritual climates attract certain spirits allowed by unchallenged, established foundations of unrighteousness, such as freemasonry. One of the chief means through which satan contends for destinies of nations is by disabling and distracting the Church where possible, through incessant spiritual attacks, including sickness, unemployment, stress, and discouragement.

Contending With the Elymas Spirit

Jesus taught about an internal spiritual source of power, not an external kingdom to come (see John 17:21). Paul warned that the Kingdom of God was not in word, but in the manifesting power thereof (see 1 Cor. 4:20). He also testified to the expression of the Kingdom in demonstration of the Spirit and of power (see 1 Cor. 2:4). The Kingdom of God is inside of you, a fact that satan hates; and his wish is that you forget this important key of your inheritance in Christ. To guarantee success in the spiritual battles of today necessitates a lifestyle of radical holiness in the face of increasing pressure on believers.

God loves cities; hence, he has appointed you as His representative. It is evident from Bible history that demonic influences can have natural implications. For instance, the case of Elymas the sorcerer and Sergius Paulus reveals the influence of a mayor over a city, and we learn that any form of deception in the lives of senior public officials can affect a city.

Sergius Paulus, the proconsul and "an intelligent man" (see Acts 13:7) was targeted by familiar spirits operating through Elymas. The natural implication was an unsaved city mayor in close relationship with a false prophet (see Acts 13:4-12). It was the responsibility of the early Church to set Sergius Paulus free from deception. Consequently, Saul (also called Paul) and his travelling party *"being sent out by the*

Holy Spirit" (Acts 13:4a) were divinely directed to a city controlled by a strongman operating through Elymas. Saul was chosen to engage with the familiar spirit having territorial influence over the island of Cyprus. He was *"filled with the Holy Spirit"* (Acts 13:9b) to confront a principality or spirit that was operating through human access with obvious natural implications.

Saul said, *"O full of all deceit and all fraud, you son of the devil, you enemy of all righteousness, will you not cease perverting the straight ways of the Lord?"* (Acts 13:10).

Considering Saul's Holy Spirit-inspired speech, one may safely deduce that spirit beings operating through humans can hold entire cities bondage. But permit my indulgence in desiring to understand how an intelligent city mayor of influence could come under the influence of Elymas of lesser intelligence.

Understanding Spiritual Warfare

This book, *Breaking the Bonds of Wickedness in the Last Days*, aims to inform believers of some emerging spiritual trends, and I will attempt to draw attention to parallels also patterned in the Bible. Unless those who are privileged to teach and preach biblical accounts accommodate perspectives uncommon to their experience, the Body of Christ may compromise her stewardship responsibilities. We need to welcome understandings from other cultures in our diverse world. I offer this suggestion due to the need to accurately interpret physical manifestations of obvious spiritual maneuvers beyond our Western minds.

One Bible account of Jesus casting out demons should not elicit countless interpretations; but as Martin Scott writes, "We have to acknowledge that those who both seek to follow Jesus and be obedient to Scripture don't always come to the same conclusion."[3] So, it may be the case that common understanding of demonology for ease of interpretation is necessary if we are to advance the Kingdom of Heaven. Revelation is progressive and also necessary for effectiveness in strategic level spiritual warfare. Martin Scott highlighted this fact

Spiritual War

in his book, *Sowing Seeds for Revival*, renamed *Gaining Grounds*. He said, "Revelation is essential, for through revelation we connect with Heaven and the resources of Heaven are unlocked to us. If this is true then without revelation effective prayer is impossible."[4]

Jesus Christ's ministry involved setting captives free from demon possession, and when He did, true freedom came to those He encountered. The early Church followed the same pattern as seen in the case of Elymas the sorcerer in Acts 13 and the little girl with the spirit of divination in Acts 16. My understanding of spiritual warfare has not been without controversy as I have struggled to balance my inner fears and the differing opinions around me. I write from a perspective of someone who while not being a doubter chose not to be a practitioner. I simply had no desire to gain knowledge or understanding of spiritual wars in invisible realms, although I quoted Scriptures referring to such wars, like other believers did. Now I share the following opinion of a respected friend to support the message of this book: We cannot decide to be involved in warfare; we have been committed to war. Either we will be effective and take ground, or we will be ineffective, neither exercising authority for ourselves or on behalf of others in setting them free.[5]

Testing Versus Temptation

Even though many people may not admit it, they continue to blame the devil for most difficulties, as I have pointed out in previous chapters. But not all afflictions are from the devil. God does allow us to go through processes of spiritual maturity for His own glory. *"But we all, with unveiled face, beholding as in a mirror the glory of the Lord, are being transformed into the same image from glory to glory, just as by the Spirit of the Lord"* (2 Cor. 3:18). God may test His children, but He will not tempt. Temptations are of the devil, intended for destruction:

> *Let no one say when he is tempted, "I am tempted by God"; for God cannot be tempted by evil, nor does He Himself tempt anyone* (James 1:13).

On the other hand, sin exposes believers to temptation—*"But each one is tempted when he is drawn away by his own desires and enticed"* (James 1:14). Righteous seeds bring about righteous harvest, but sin gives birth to death; hence, believers need to break unrighteous covenants, treaties, or agreements covering the foundation of their lives (see James 1:15).

A person who honors the Lord and His Word and loves his fellow beings is a holy person in right standing with God; *"But as He who called you is holy, you also be holy in all your conduct, because it is written, 'Be holy, for I am holy'"* (1 Pet. 1:15-16).

As you pray the suggested prayers in this section, you will learn to set boundaries around your life with the blood of Jesus. You will hopefully adopt a practice of prayerfully placing your situations before God and to pray without ceasing. The process of elimination in getting to the root of a problem necessitates violent prayers that I have also proposed in this section. They are only suggested prayers and not to be substituted for the Holy Spirit's voice of direction while you pray.

Spiritual Wars

Spiritual wars are against:

- Principalities and powers.
- The rulers of the darkness of this age.
- Spiritual hosts of wickedness in the heavenly places (see Eph. 6:12).

The term *spiritual warfare* refers to invisible wars fought with unseen weapons against invisible enemies—satan and his cohorts. An experienced apostle of distinction cautions those who must fight the spiritual wicked forces against the Church and writes, "Satan and the demons under his control are real beings with warped personalities, wicked hearts and malicious intents."[6]

Hence, battles are won only by committed and persistent prayers. Satan's aim is to interfere with the manifestation of the Kingdom of God through His people. God's Kingdom is inside of you waiting to be displayed through your resilience to adversity. You are therefore to refrain from giving the devil publicity he craves by declaring your weakness in trials. Because spiritual warfare is not fought with humans nor with natural weapons, I have included insight and prayers as the most potent weapons.

The devil has long appeared to be winning in his warfare against the Church, but he is a liar. In order to reinforce the devil's defeat at Calvary, a conscious decision is required on your part to prepare for the wars of our time. I personally believe, as the Lord revealed to my heart, that there is a strong need to break bonds of wickedness or unholy alliances that are weakening our fighting army. Can we continue to battle someone who is our master? Romans 6:16 points out absolute folly in such a practice:

Do you not know that to whom you present yourselves slaves to obey, you are that one's slaves whom you obey, whether of sin leading to death, or of obedience leading to righteousness?

Serving sin denies a believer the authority to fight against sin. When engaging in strategic level spiritual warfare or advanced level spiritual combat, it is important to think and speak positive words of faith. Puffing up the devil by our words or giving the devil credit for any difficulty may create the impression of his importance or false awe. With this truth in mind, you cannot then afford to *"war according to the flesh"* (2 Cor. 10:3b). But as a child of the living God, you are to fight with weapons that are *"mighty in God"* (2 Cor. 10:4b) for...

- Pulling down strongholds.
- Casting down arguments.
- Casting down every high thing that exalts itself against the knowledge of God.
- Bringing every thought into captivity to the obedience of Christ (see 2 Cor. 10:4-5).

Consistent, righteous prayers yield God-ordained results. Without prayer, we are impotent in our struggle with the enemy.[7]

The Weapon of Sacrificial Giving

My perspective of spiritual warfare was affected by another incident in a season of revelation. While on a private visit to Nigeria, Africa, in November 2004, I received a telephone call during the early hours of one morning. I recognized my caller as the husband of a dear prophetic pastor who I had felt a sense of commitment to support in January, earlier that same year. I had not known the lady, but was blessed by her potent apostolic and prophetic ministry. The accuracy of the words she spoke by way of prophetic utterance made one prostrate before God for His manifold gifts in the Body of Christ. I then felt led of the Spirit of the Lord to sow a seed toward rent for a more comfortable home for her, although I had only just met her.

The Lord also impressed upon my heart to open doors to her to speak to some senior government officials. During the short space of time after I had met the lady, I was led of the Lord to sacrifice time, money, and other material possessions. I did not know the Lord was actually giving me an opportunity to be saved by prayers of the prophetess later on in the same year.

My frantic caller, the husband of this dear lady, asked if I knew of a man whom he named, and I said that he had been a former employee of mine. He said he had to break protocol to inform me of a dialogue between his wife and the family of my former employee. Under a bogus claim in classic Balaam style, the prophetess had been solicited to pray against an employer. When my name was given on a piece of paper to the prophetess, my sacrificial giving in the same year yeilded good harvest like Issac in Genesis 26:12, speaking for me like an altar. The prophetess informed her shocked visitors that she knew the person in question. She spoke as one who had stood with me in prayer through the past year and was able to debunk their claims. She informed her born-again Christian visitors seeking prayer agreement against me that I had paid her rent for the home they were now sitting in, making an unrighteous request. Sacrificial giving to a person I hardly knew served as leverage for protection from fiery darts of the enemy. My mind-set changed and so did my heart. Consequently, my worship of the Almighty who watches over our predetermined course increased.

Satanic Arrows Are Diverted

I was initially shocked and fearful, but thoughts of God's amazing grace left me in awe of His goodness. How could it be that a token seed could direct fiery darts of the enemy to a safe ground where they could be destroyed by the power of prayer? The Lord of Hosts diverted dangerous Balaamic arrows of divination to the only prophetess I knew in a nation of over one hundred fifty million people.

I began inquiring of the Lord, seeking to understand how a believer can be successfully cursed by other humans. My mother who was a committed intercessor and close friend to the Lord had told me compromise could open the door for satan's arrows, whereas righteousness shut doors in the face of the enemy.

My concern waned to some degree when the Lord reminded me of His covenant of protection over His servant (see Isa. 54:17). Standing in the righteousness of God will protect you from satanic arrows. The blood of Jesus will divert such evil arrows to be destroyed. How could the Lord have diverted an arrow of accusation to the only prophetess I knew in a vast nation I did not even live in? This rhetorical question remains a focus of amazement and awe.

Pray...

- Thank You, Lord, that when the enemy comes at me like a flood, Your Spirit raises a standard against him (see Isa. 59:19).
- Thank You, Lord, for when the enemy subverts my cause without Your permission, You will nullify his evil decrees, laws, and bylaws against my destiny (see Lam. 3:35-37).
- Thank You, Lord, for even in trials You have caused me to walk in my high places (see Hab. 3:19).

In Jesus' name I have prayed, Amen.

ENDNOTES

1. Quin Sherrer and Ruthanne Garlock, *A Woman's Guide to Breaking Bondages* (Annarbor, MI: Servant Publications, 1994) p. 16.
2. Ibid, p.16.
3. Martin Scott, *Sowing Seeds for Revival*, republished under the new title *Gaining Grounds* (Tonbridge, Kent: Sovereign World, 2001) p. 29.
4. Ibid, p. 29.
5. Ibid, p. 45.
6. C. Peter Wagner, *Territorial Spirits* (Tonbridge, Kent: Sovereign World, 1991) p. 7.
7. Ibid, p. 8.

PRAYER SECTION 2

The Battle Belongs to the Lord

The Church has been given responsibility to make the manifold wisdom of Christ Jesus known to principalities and powers in heavenly places (see Eph. 3:10).

The Greek word *polupoikilos*, which translates "manifold" means "multifaceted; varied; multidimensional." God's wisdom is multifaceted. It is important, therefore, that you do not limit yourself to past or familiar knowledge and experience. The Church body is to manifest God's greatness on the earth; *"For the earnest expectation of the creation eagerly waits for the revealing of the sons of God"* (Rom. 8:19). In doing so, principalities and powers in heavenly places will be frustrated and their evil devices brought to nought (see Isa. 44:24-25).

Spiritual wars are best fought and won in the heavenly places. Such wars are not fought with visible armies such as we see in the Iraqi war, but against invisible spirit beings with evil agendas. Yet often, believers battle problems on a physical level by talking about the same conditions, or worse, speaking God's Word without accompanying faith. Consider the two tribes who were commended for their part in Deborah's army: *"Zebulun is a people who jeopardized their lives to the point of death, Naphtali also, on the heights of the battlefield"* (Judg. 5:18). The earth is to host manifestations of victories in the heavenly realms. Kings also fought in the fierce war of Deborah and Barak: *"They fought from the heavens; the stars from their courses fought against Sisera"* (Judg. 5:20). Men of Naphtali were those who knew how to fight from heights downward.

Ephesians 3:10 is only achievable when you receive revelation of your new identity as a new creation in Christ Jesus. The Bible reveals the new status gained by born-again Christians:

> *Therefore, if anyone is in Christ, he is a new creation; old things have passed away; behold, all things have become new* (2 Corinthians 5:17).

Satan hates to be reminded of your new identity, so instead, he accuses your past or present status. His aim in accusing the brethren is to compromise their future as he did with the first Adam. And because satan is the accuser of the brethren and a liar, it is important that you remind him of his fate as you pray.

Maintaining Focus

Abraham received a promise for himself and his descendants, and part of the promise was the ability to "possess the gate of the enemy" (see Gen. 22:17). You, likewise, as a descendant of Abraham also are blessed with anointing to subdue the enemy in his evil agendas. Jesus promised to build His Church; and the gates of hell will not prevail or resist advancement of any Church built on the revelation of Jesus Christ as the Lord (see Matt. 16:18). You are a soldier at war with an unrepentant enemy who is instructed to interrupt future plans. As satan persists in executing well-planned evil agendas, the Bible warns you to keep focused:

The Battle Belongs to the Lord

No one engaged in warfare entangles himself with the affairs of this life, that he may please him who enlisted him as a soldier (2 Timothy 2:4).

As believers in Christ Jesus, we are not to be entangled with affairs of this world that can so easily distract. On the contrary, we are to set our eyes on the Lord as flint (see Isa. 50:7). It should also be important to a believer's military outlook that proper uniforms are worn for spiritual battles, for soldiers do not go to war in casual clothes. Military uniforms identify soldiers and their ranks.

In order to engage in the spiritual wars of the day, you will also need to look inward to examine your existing armor of warfare. When God was going to war to battle for justice for Zion, He dressed specifically for war:

He put on righteousness as a breastplate, and a helmet of salvation on His head; He put on the garments of vengeance for clothing, and was clad with zeal as a cloak (Isaiah 59:17).

Your eyes must be set firmly on the Lord at all times regardless of the pressures around. I once had a friend who sensationalized spiritual warfare to a point of irritation to my spirit. He simply never took responsibilities for human failings; instead, he gave the devil credit for everything that went wrong around him. I found myself saying to this friend that if the devil was so powerful and able to disrupt life when and where he wanted, then what exactly is the point of being a Christian? I tend to offend believers who do not like confronting truth with transparency. We must avoid people who inadvertently lock our minds in negativity and then silence us with religiosity. Such people deny others opportunity to question their out-of-balance theology.

My commission expressed through the pages of this book is to challenge Christians to live their lives worthy of the sacrifice of Christ's life. Unless we believers proactively seek the Lord to reveal unrighteous foundations in our lives and cut the supply source feeding unrighteousness, we will be in trouble.

Warring Winner

As I continue to emphasize through the pages of this book, spiritual wars are not fought against flesh and blood, but against defeated enemies, such as poverty, sickness, disease, and immorality. Jesus Christ, in His obedience by offering His life as a sacrifice for reconciliation, armed the Church with the weapon of His blood.

> *Having wiped out the handwriting of requirements that was against us, which was contrary to us. And He has taken it out of the way, having nailed it to the cross. Having disarmed principalities and powers, He made a public spectacle of them, triumphing over them in it* (Colossians 2:14-15).

To win the wars of our time, believers must be appropriately dressed and wearing the proper uniforms. We are also to put on the full armor of God in order to stand in the day of adversity:

> *Finally, my brethren, be strong in the Lord and in the power of His might. Put on the whole armor of God, that you may be able to stand against the wiles of the devil* (Ephesians 6:10-11).

The psalmist concluded, "*Now I know that the Lord saves His anointed*" (Ps. 20:6a).

The Lord has saved you from every trick the enemy could possibly have up his sleeves. It is my prayer that you will concur, praying with the conviction of the psalmist.

Breaking the Bonds and Declaring the Victory

Jesus taught that attempting to take over the goods of a strongman without first binding the strongman is futile. So, in order to help you bind the strongman, this book is to be used on two levels. In the first instance, it will help you to prepare as a soldier of Christ, and secondly, it will enable you to practice the art of warfare. Each prayer section has been divinely inspired by the Holy Spirit and is founded on the Word of God.

The devil would rather believers prayed in ignorance, instead of with apostolic authority. But with authority, you will declare a word in prayer, and it shall be established on your behalf and those you stand for (see Job 22:28).

Many believers today find it difficult to comprehend that Paul cursed the spirit in Elymas. But unless evil powers controlling lives of humans, even believers who are in compromise, are nullified, the Church will continue to face challenges to her authority. Indeed, we cannot fight with part of our army in bondage or constantly drawn into unnecessary spiritual warfare.

A common practice in a natural war is for a military force to apply strategies carefully formulated by senior officers. Such strategies usually put together by generals of a national force are then followed by every arm of the forces.

The prayers you are about to read and hopefully embrace as your own are targeted at preparing you for victory in the evil day at hand (see Eph. 6:13). For so long, the devil has accused believers with past issues, creating present problems with future implications. And unless believers now sort out foundations of their lives, the devil will carry on his agenda of discreditment. He is a liar and deceiver, and there is no truth in his mouth (see John 10:10).

When Roman officials sought to confine the early Church, the saints gathered to pray to God. The Bible records:

And when they had prayed, the place where they were assembled together was shaken; and they were all filled with the Holy Spirit, and they spoke the word of God with boldness (Acts 4:31).

The force of their prayer of faith caused the ground to respond.

The foundation or base of your life, which could be likened to the earth's soil, receives covenants or agreements made on your behalf or made by yourself. Bonds of wickedness or demonic covenants can cause stagnancy in a person's spiritual growth, ultimately affecting natural abilities. Another implication of attempting to lead a full life without ridding oneself of unrighteous foundations is a state of spiritual impotence. Many in the Body of Christ are aware of God's power

BREAKING the BONDS of Wickedness *in* the Last *Days*

to save, heal, and deliver; yet so many of our soldiers experience great opposition when attempting to outwork the promises of God for their lives. One important key to enjoying true freedom in Christ is to break the bonds of wickedness in your life.

I do not believe, however, that my call or your call is to stay in incessant spiritual battles; rather, we are to worship the Lord our God with all our hearts. When using these prayers, it is important to submit and to surrender your spiritual battles to the Lord. You do so mentally by believing the Lord is able to take care of any situation you talk to Him about and then physically follow through, matching words with actions of faith. No one knows you better than the Lord your God who seeks true worship from you (see John 4:24). He is interested in seeing you fulfill your destiny, and in order to do so, you must approach His throne in hope while speaking words of your prayers.

Pray...

- Lord, I thank You, for the battle belongs to You (see 2 Chron. 20:15).
- Thank You, Lord, for You are with me. Who then can be against me? (see Rom. 8:31).
- Thank You, Lord, that even though the enemy's weapons have formed against me, they shall not prosper, as Your Word declares (see Isa. 54:17).
- Thank You, Lord, for granting me peace in adversity. I will now wait until my change comes (see Job 14:14).

In Jesus' name I have prayed, Amen.

Now prepare yourself to engage with some rules of the present-day war of the Church.

PRAYER SECTION 3

Dressed for War

The Bible warns us to put on the full armor of God, especially when engaging in spiritual warfare.

> *Finally, my brethren, be strong in the Lord and in the power of His might. Put on the whole armor of God, that you may be able to stand against the wiles of the devil. For we do not wrestle against flesh and blood, but against principalities, against powers, against the rulers of the darkness of this age, against spiritual hosts of wickedness in the heavenly places. Therefore take up the whole armor of God, that you may be able to withstand in the evil day, and having done all, to stand. Stand therefore, having girded your waist with truth, having put on the breastplate of righteousness, and having your feet shod with the preparation of the gospel of peace; above all, taking the shield of faith with which you will be able to quench all the fiery darts of the wicked one. And take the helmet of salvation, and the sword of the*

> Spirit, which is the word of God; praying always with all prayer and supplication in the Spirit, being watchful to this end with all perseverance and supplication for all the saints (Ephesians 6:10-18).

As mentioned previously, when God dressed up as a Commander in Chief to win justice for Zion, He was so determined to win justice for His people that He put on zeal as an outer garment. The Good News version of the Bible translates *zeal* as *"a strong desire to set things right"* (see Isa. 59:17).

God Dresses for Justice

I once had a dream after crying out to the Lord trying to make sense of a difficult situation where I felt particularly mistreated. I was taken up to Heaven and ushered straight into the throne room of God. He sat at a table as the President of a country familiar to me in the natural. I later realized the president of that country is also known as "the commander in chief" of the national forces. A black, old-fashioned telephone sat on His table. I recognized the black telephone as one in which God had used to speak to me on rare occasions.

I had previously had two dreams where God's voice came to me through the black telephone; one dream was about a woman who was known internationally as a prophetess and was called upon to answer the black telephone. The Lord used the dream channel to introduce the lady and her value in Heaven to me (see 2 Cor. 5:16).

God, represented in the image or person of an earthly president, asked me to sit on a seat opposite Him as He answered other complaints coming through on the black telephone from His children who were suffering injustices. As a child of the living God, you can dial straight through to His telephone line with the words of your prayers. I watched as He personally took note of the details of telephone calls put through to His direct line. He then got up after taking a call from a lady in Iceland and another in Alaska whose carpet shop had burned down. When He returned, I asked why He was dressed like an Alaskan. He was carrying a steel camping thermos as well. He said He needed to dress for the weather of the Alaskans. I was very fascinated and had stopped crying by this time. I then asked one of the angels nearby if I could buy the same flask. When he told me how much it would cost, I responded that I could get one in England for 50 pounds.

I continued to wait patiently for my turn, fully assured of God's strong desire to give justice to His children. Later, the Spirit of the Lord began to interpret my experience and to teach me what every aspect of my journey to God's "Department of Justice" in Heaven meant. I had seen the substance of Isaiah 59:16-20. In order to solve the problems coming through to God's special table, He had to identify with not only the problems but also the spiritual climate where the injustice was taking place. I resolved in my heart not to ever seek my own justice but to live my life in God's ordained will so that my telephone calls could be put through to His direct line. God's desire was to identify with every aspect of the caller's life, including wearing the appropriate clothing for the peculiar weather in Alaska.

Indeed, the blood of Jesus has won justice for every born-again child of God (see Col. 2:14-15). So now, every man created has been given opportunity to receive the free gift of salvation. Those who do receive Christ are to walk faithfully before Him. Others choosing to oppose God's will by colluding with demonic agents to disrupt lives of other believers should be stopped by the army of God. In warring against the enemy's devices, the believer is to war with hope, engaging in "the good warfare" (see 1 Tim. 1:18). God's will and plan for your life is clearly defined in His holy Word. It is for this reason that your counteroffensive against the enemy is "the good warfare"—war with a predetermined outcome of victory for you as a believer in Christ Jesus. While we are not to covet spiritual warfare or even live our lives expecting warfare, at the same time it is unacceptable when the devil crosses his boundary by placing a child of God in a cycle of defeat where meaningless struggles start to occur.

The Weapons Against You

We are beneficiaries of a covenant promise which says, "*No weapon formed against you shall prosper*" (Isa. 54:17a). To ensure that evil weapons are defeated even after being formed, we must break the bonds of wickedness and proactively live right by God. Believers are familiar with the "one step forward and two steps backward" syndrome—a lie of the enemy. Now is the time to solidify foundations of your life, by breaking demonic covenants that fertilize the ground of our lives.

The purpose of the prayers in this book is to help you deal with foundational sin and spiritual encumbrances. Unresolved issues, spiritual or natural, can serve as entry points or points of contact for demonic scud missiles to be fired at you or at your family. But regardless of your present difficulties, it is important to have your mind ruled by the Word of God and be reminded that *"no weapon formed against you shall prosper."* The Lord spoke to me intermittently but consistently about a weapon that was forming against my family, and He promised that the weapon would be formed but it would not prosper. True to the exact warning of the Lord, the weapon formed but did not prosper.

As a servant of the Lord, you have received the promise of divine protection as a heritage, your inheritance, and realize that every challenge encountered by a child of God is not to be interpreted as a work of the devil. God said, *"Behold, I have refined you, but not as silver; I have tested you in the furnace of affliction"* (Ps. 48:10). It is important, therefore, to interpret your experiences before giving the devil credit for a refining process. God's refining process is a blessing. The Word of God assures us that His blessing makes His children rich, and He adds no sorrows with it (see Prov. 10:22).

When God tests His children, the testing is undergirded by His grace, which makes such experiences bearable. Hence, you are to count it joy when you go through various trials knowing that the testing of your faith will produce patience (see James 1:3). The Bible rewards faithfulness in the Lord's testing with "perfect and complete, lacking nothing" (James 1:4b). God tempts no one; therefore, the devil is to be held responsible for temptations you and other believers endure (see James 1:13).

Effective, Fervent Prayer

Unless patterns around your life are carefully examined with a goal to breaking demonic trends, prayer will only keep you safe but not delivered. Therefore, strategic prayers should be undertaken with optimism and a view to bring demonic sieges, which drain spiritual energy, to an end. You are within your God-given rights to challenge patterns and cycles that mock God's promises for your life. If a natural father promises one thing and something else manifests, a child would naturally go back to his father to ask questions. Born-again Christians or believers do endure unpleasant experiences as the Bible records: *"Many are the afflictions of the righteous, but the Lord delivers him out of them all"* (Ps. 34:19).

In the natural context, many say that experience is often the best teacher; this is also true for spiritual matters. Overcoming satanic sieges launched through past family covenants or present sin will make you a stronger, more confident Christian. Once demonic weapons, such as sickness, divorce, financial difficulty, infertility, and other challenges are identified, the next step is to avert plans of the enemy to use such weapons against you or anyone else. You are to launch a counterattack with the Word of God covering the area or subject of temptation (see Ps. 119:9). Jesus Christ spoke of the mind-set with which divine authority is to be expressed. He taught, *"And from the days of John the Baptist until now the kingdom of Heaven suffers violence, and the violent take it by force"* (Matt. 11:12). It will take a committed, tenacious, and determined mind-set to carry out a strategy of war against satanic agendas. There is no other way to evict demons other than through effective, fervent prayer. The Bible emphasizes the importance of consistency in praying:

The effective, fervent prayer of a righteous man avails much (James 5:16).

Spiritual warfare is not a dreamed-up episode of "Star Wars" but a serious reality the Church must address (see 1 Pet. 5:8-9) There is a need to violently declare your inheritance and a right to retain your due blessings as a believer in Christ Jesus. Likewise, it is important to be appropriately dressed and armed to go to war against satanic ambushes and to destroy evil structures operating against your life and that of your family.

Declare...

- I am strong in the Lord and in the power of His might.
- I now put on the whole armor of God, and I shall stand against the wiles of the enemy working against my destiny.
- I have girded my waist with truth.
- I have put on the breastplate of righteousness.
- I have shod my feet with the preparation of the gospel of peace.
- I have taken up the shield of faith, and by it I shall quench the fiery darts of the wicked one.
- I have taken up my helmet of salvation.
- I have taken up the Sword of the Spirit, which is the Word of God (see Eph. 6:14-17).
- I know this battle belongs to the Lord and so I shall not fear (see 1 Sam. 17:47).

In Jesus' name, Amen.

PRAYER SECTION 4

The Weapon of the Word of God

Forever, O Lord, Your word is settled in Heaven (Psalm 119:89).

Soldiers of the Lord are to be armed at all times with the infallible Word of God. The Word of God is a weapon of offense with which spiritual wars against His children are won. It is important to remind yourself of some of the attributes of the Word of God for your encouragement. The psalmist reminds us that the way to keep on the right path is to take heed of the Word of God (see Ps. 119:9). When our hearts become storehouses able to hold the secrets of the Lord, we can then abstain from sin which entraps (see Ps. 119:11). God's Word is God (see John 1:1), and God desires that His children apply the full force and power of His Word to advance His Kingdom on earth (see Matt. 11:11-12).

Jesus Christ Himself defeated satan with the written Word of God, and on one occasion, He reminded him, *"It is written, 'Man shall not* live by bread alone, but by every word of God'" (Luke 4:4). In his continued ignorance, satan then tried to offer the Lord Jesus riches that were His in the first place (see Luke 4:7). I have discovered in my prayer life that any prayer not founded on the Word of God is weightless before the enemy. God's Word is complete (see Ps. 12:6; Rev. 22:18) and sufficient for every experience, so we are to use it extensively. With the Word of God, we are able to quench fiery darts of the enemy (see Eph. 6:16-17), and with the Word of God, we are able to release the destiny of a people and a nation (see Exod. 3:10). It is on the Word and by the Word of God that a believer can stand to win spiritual battles of our time (see 1 Kings 17:1).

Jesus, in praying to His Father for His disciples, said, "*I have given them Your word; and the world has hated them because they are not of this world, just as I am not of the world*" (see John 17:14). So, in effect, the Word of God shapes and forms our lives and delivers us from conformity to shapes, patterns, and models of the world. But as long as our appearance is like those of the world, change will elude the Church (see Rom. 12:1-2). I urge you to meditate on some attributes of God's Word listed below.

God's Word [is]...

- Truth (see John 17:17).
- Infallible (see Isa. 55:11).
- Pure (see Ps. 119:140).
- Instructs in righteousness (see Ps. 119:9).
- Guards against sin (see Ps. 119:11).
- Strengthens the soul (see Ps. 119:28).
- Revives the soul (see Ps. 119:25).
- Settled in Heaven (see Ps. 119:89).
- Breaks rocks into pieces (see Jer. 23:29).
- Stands forever (see 1 Pet. 1:25).
- Like fire (see Jer. 23:29).
- A burning fire shut up in the bones (see Jer. 20:9).

The Weapon of the Word of God

- Guarantees breakthrough (see Isa. 55:11).
- Like silver purified seven times (see Ps. 12:6).
- The word of truth (see Ps. 119:43).
- Our hope (see Ps. 119:49).
- Gives life (see Ps. 119:50).
- Sweeter than honey (see Ps. 119:103).
- Lightens our paths (Ps. 119:105).
- A gateway to understanding (see Ps. 119:130).
- Guides our lives (see Ps. 119:133).
- Distinguishes your life (see John 17:14).

Using the Word, it is important to break demonic agreements working against your life and challenging your destiny. Covenants that now strengthen satan's resolve should be broken and destroyed with potent prayers and proclamations from the Word. Although blinded by evil, the devil still recognizes the importance of contractual terms, and he understands the power of agreements, so he initiates his evil agreements placing them on platforms from where attacks are launched at believers. He seeks agreement with believers by deceiving some into believing his lies. He then attempts to harvest seeds of evil agreements already functioning in lives through original lies seeded into foundations.

Pray...

- Thank You, Lord, for Your Word is a two-edged sword, with which I shall overcome every demonic agenda targeting my life (see Heb. 4:12).
- Thank You, Lord, for Your Word; I shall arise to terrorize the devil and his evil cohorts warring against my destiny (see Zech. 1:21).
- Thank You, Lord, for Your Word; I shall arise this day to cut into pieces every agent of satan attacking my purpose. *"For the word of God is living and powerful"* (Heb. 4:12a).

- Thank You, Lord, for Your Word; I shall arm myself with the Sword of the Spirit to slay every spiritual giant challenging God's will for my life (see 1 Sam. 17:49).
- Thank You, Lord, for Your Word; I shall advance with faith and assurance in the promises of God for my life (see Rom. 1:17).
- Thank You, Lord, for Your Word, for I know You have heard my cries (see Jer. 33:3).
- Thank You, Lord, for Your Word; I know You will honor Your Word in my life.

In Jesus' name, Amen.

PRAYER SECTION 5

The Weapon of the Blood of Jesus

Bows and arrows in modern-day wars such as the Iraq war would obviously leave an army totally defeated. Rather, natural wars are fought with weapons suitable to the particular war at hand, including man-made or manufactured weapons such as rifles, fighter jets, bombs, or even nuclear weapons. Spiritual wars, likewise, require appropriate weapons, with a mind-set of victory in order to defeat the enemy. They are to be fought and won with weapons that are mighty in God. Moreover, the blood of Jesus is the Church's most potent and effective weapon of spiritual warfare (see Col. 2:14-15).

The Covenant Blood Severs Links With Evil

The devil hates to be reminded of the power in the blood of Jesus, and when you declare the blood to spirit beings in dreams, for instance, they react by fleeing with fear. It is important to remember that the overcoming party in the Book of Revelation withstood lucifer and his fallen angels (see Rev. 12:11). Even while satan is an accuser of the brethren who specializes in reminding people of their past compromises and sin, this prayer book encourages you to prepare for spiritual wars of our time by adequately severing links with bonds of wickedness in your life, family line, or through relationships. Sex, for instance, is a sacred experience bonding two people in a blessed union before God; but when perverted, the act of sex can also bind two people in bonds of wickedness, even transferring family line curses from one person to another. The Lord showed me that this occurs by creating *access* or an *opening* through which spirits in one party's personal or family line are able to track the other party to a relationship.

Sex outside of marriage amounts to fornication and adultery, both regarded by the Bible as sin. Such agreements, whether innocent or not, bear spiritual implications that could create access for demonic forces to wage wars of accusation and so forth against you. The essence of the blood covenant is the amazing grace we as born-again Christians now have to humbly receive inspiration from the Holy Spirit regarding "the weight" or sin that ensnares us. The Holy Spirit at every level of spiritual development and growth warns His children of unresolved issues in our lives that could be strengthening the devil against us. A child of God who continues to reject the power of the blood of Jesus to deal with past, present, and future issues or remains ignorant to its saving grace may find his or her life placed under demonic sieges. By demonic siege, I refer to a pattern of accusation where you hear the same lies told in your ears reminding you of that relationship that you regret having in the first place. Satan will win in his war to oppress if you receive and believe his lies about past sexual partners. And he will continue to succeed if you do not wage a good warfare for your future by praying Scriptures such as Second Corinthians 5:17 that remind us of the truth:

Therefore, if anyone is in Christ, he is a new creation; old things have passed away; behold, all things have become new.

Overcoming by the Blood

God has reconciled you to Himself through Jesus Christ (see 2 Cor. 5:18), and has now given you a new ministry of reconciliation. You

The Weapon of the Blood of Jesus

have a destiny and destiny is what the devil dreads. Your destiny is to bring change in your sphere of influence. *Destiny is about achieving a predetermined course of events*; hence, the devil employs accusations of past wrongs to compromise future advancements. You should exercise your divine rights to make peace with the Lord for past sin rather than allow the devil to judge your future accomplishments. The verdict before the shedding of the blood of Jesus for your sake was: *"For all have sinned and fall short of the glory of God"* (Rom. 3:23). But now the blood of Jesus has changed all of that, and the verdict reads thus: *"There is therefore now no condemnation to those who are in Christ Jesus"* (Rom. 8:1a).

Hence, you are to boldly approach the Lord in your time of prayer (see Heb. 4:16), and to seek Him for revelation of past and entrenched sin that now compromises your future (see Jer. 33:3). A strong understanding of the blood covenant and importance of Jesus Christ's sacrifice at Calvary is absolutely crucial for your complete freedom from oppression. You are special to the Lord. Your life deserves to be led without trauma of past issues springing up to challenge future aspirations. You are the righteousness of Christ; *"For He made Him who knew no sin to be sin for us, that we might become the righteousness of God in Him"* (2 Cor. 5:21).

You have been justified freely by God's grace through redemption that is in Christ Jesus (see Rom. 3:24). Christ, the Anointed One, shed His blood to pay a complete price for your past, present, and future (see Heb. 9:12). But unless you redeem your inheritance, the funds remain in a trust account, like money in the bank. A prayer warrior without understanding of the power of the blood of Jesus is like a toddler trying to crash into adult conversation. But know that you are free of accusations! The blood of Jesus is your weapon of war having redeemed you totally from every accusation of the enemy as the Bible confirms: *"…without shedding of blood there is no remission"* (Heb. 9:22).

Revelation 12 tells of a war that will break out in Heaven between Michael, other angels, and the great fiery dragon. A group is mentioned as those who overcome by the "blood of the Lamb." You too can win with the blood of Jesus. All you need to do is pick up a powerful weapon which many have dropped or forgotten. Prophetically engaging with the Lord and His plans for your life is the only way of gaining total freedom to enjoy life as a new person in Christ. When Samson laid down the strategy of God (jaw bone) with which he slew a thousand Philistines, he then grew thirsty (see Judg. 15:17-19). But even then, God opened a hollow place to release water for Samson's revival.

As the Body of Christ is now confronted with the reality of intensified spiritual warfare, Christian soldiers ought to be familiar with the most potent weapon of this present-day war.

And they overcame him by the blood of the Lamb and by the word of their testimony, and they did not love their lives to the death (Revelation 12:11).

Offer Thanksgiving...

- Thank You, Lord, that by Your blood I have inherited boldness and access with confidence through faith in You (see Eph. 2:18; 3:12; Heb. 4:16).
- Thank You, Lord, that in Your blood I choose to enter into Your gates with thanksgiving and into Your courts with praise (see Ps. 100:4).
- Thank You, Lord, for in Your blood I can now come before Your throne of grace with boldness and hope (see Heb. 4:16).
- Thank You, Lord, for in Your blood I am assured of mercy and I shall find grace to help in time of need (see Heb. 4:16).
- I am thankful to You, Lord, and I bless Your name. In Jesus' name, Amen.

Pray Against Condemnation...

- Thank You, Lord, that I can come before You, not in my own righteousness, but in the righteousness gained through Your blood (see Eph. 2:18).

- Thank You, Lord, for the blessings of Your Word (see Heb. 4:12).
- Thank You, Lord, for the sacrifice of Your life at Calvary, which makes me a beneficiary of promises in Your blood.
- Thank You, Lord, for the power in Your blood available to me.
- Thank You, Lord, for benefits of Your blood, which make me a beneficiary of unmerited favor.
- Thank You, Lord, for the gains in Your blood, which include freedom for my life.
- Thank You, Lord, for victory in Your blood, which makes me not only a conqueror but more than a conqueror.
- Thank You, Lord, for breakthrough in Your blood, which makes me confident when I pray.

Now Pray...

I thank You, Lord, for offering Your life for me on the cross at Calvary. Forgive me, Lord, for not honoring Your sacrifice and deliver me from all evil. I now surrender my cares to You as I pray in Jesus' name, Amen.

THE BLOOD OF JESUS SPEAKS

Calling for Justice in Times of Trouble

When facing trials, tribulations, and temptations, it is important not to seek your own justice or to war for your own vindication. Your focus must remain on Jesus Christ, *"...the author and finisher of our faith..."* (Heb. 12:2a). If care is not taken, it is quite easy to fall into the temptation of justifying oneself, even to the detriment of others.

The Holy Spirit once taught me a powerful lesson on prayer when I was at a low ebb in ministry. I was led to understand that some of the most powerful prayers a believer can ever utter are simply speaking Scriptures back to God. A prayer was then deposited in my heart and out of the abundance of my heart I would hear myself call out, "Lord, please don't let me fight a war You can fight for me." In effect, the Holy Spirit was leading me to pray words that revealed the folly of seeking one's own justice.

The prayers in this book were born out of personal experiences, and many of the words were received directly from the Holy Spirit. My experience in the Lord's school of prayer taught me to pray prayers that move Heaven in every circumstance. Likewise, when presenting your prayer petitions to the Lord, do so with "no strings attached." Praying from a pure, humble heart guarantees you favor from Heaven. The Word of God reminds us to *"Be holy for I am holy."* I was again reminded only recently of the potency of Jesus Christ's shed blood. The Lord spoke words I will never forget right into my heart: *"You have known what it is like to use My blood, to apply My blood, to call for its benefits, and to honor My blood."* He continued, *"But now I want to teach you about the power of the voice of My blood."* He then revealed that the primary function of the voice of the blood of Jesus Christ is to call for justice. *Justice* here does not relate to vengeance or revenge, but justice means "your right, or entitlement." In other words, when calling for restoration of all that satan has stolen, we must deploy the voice of the blood of Jesus.

> *To Jesus the Mediator of the new covenant and to the blood of sprinkling that speaks better things than that of Abel* (Hebrews 12:24).

The voice of the blood of Jesus specifically calls for justice on behalf of His children, and the Bible acknowledges that Jesus' blood *"speaks better things than that of Abel."* Abel's blood once called for justice from the ground, after he was murdered by his immature, selfish brother Cain, for offering the Lord a worthy sacrifice.

> *By faith Abel offered to God a more excellent sacrifice than Cain, through which he obtained witness that he was righteous, God testifying of his gifts; and through it he being dead still speaks* (Hebrews 11:4).

The Weapon of the Blood of Jesus

Jealousy and envy are at the root of many evil atrocities committed by humans. Cain's spirit lives on in people who reject grace or unmerited favor offered to the human race by Jesus Christ's sacrifice of self. Cain was informed, *"The voice of your brother's blood cries out to Me from the ground"* (Gen. 4:10b). Abel's blood was calling out for justice—for his right to live, which was violently cut short. Your experience may not necessarily be that of actual murder, but of treachery, betrayal, or oppression, which can make murder seem like a more favorable experience. The result of death is cessation of life, which leaves a victim unable to feel its consequences. While, on the other hand, some of life's blows can cause prolonged hurt, pain, and wounding if the Christian does not protect his or her heart with God's Word.

The time has come to break out of cycles of disappointment to become the ambassador Christ's blood offers you as "a new person" in Him (see 2 Cor. 5:17). Breaking bonds of wickedness around and within your life will immediately propel you to a new status. A person whose life is led in righteousness of Christ, who does not seek after his own justice or vindication, is one for whom the blood of Jesus Christ will war.

The voice of the blood of Jesus is calling for better justice for you today. Furthermore, to enjoy benefits of the blood of Jesus, you need to renounce sin and break allegiances to family idolatry, which may have given satan and his coalition of demon spirits access to your life. Boldly ask the Lord to reveal areas of compromise in your life, and then call on the voice of His blood to call for your release from all forms of oppression, covenants, and curses.

Pray, Using the Voice of the Blood of Jesus...

- Thank You, Lord, that Your blood has a voice.
- Thank You, Lord, that Your blood speaks better things (calls for perfect justice) than Abel's (see Heb. 11:4).
- Thank You, Lord, that the voice of Your blood calls out from Heaven for justice on earth on my behalf (see Isa. 59:16).

- Thank You, Lord, that the voice of Your blood calls out for complete victory on my behalf.
- Thank You, Lord, for the voice of Your blood understands and knows my case and is able to plead my cause.
- I surrender my cares to You, Lord; may the voice of Your blood speak for me.
- I present my petitions before You, Lord; may the voice of Your blood speak for me.
- I lay my cause at Your table of mercy, Lord; may the voice of Your blood argue my cause.
- I lay my life at Your altar; may the voice of Your blood expose sin in my life.
- I stand in Your presence; may Your justice change my countenance as it did Hannah's.

In Jesus' name I have called. I will now wait until my change comes (see Job 14:14). Amen.

PRAYER SECTION 6

The Weapon of the Believer's Authority

New in Christ

The blood of Jesus Christ conferred a new creation status upon His followers:

> *Therefore, if any one is in Christ, he is a new creation; old things have passed away; behold, all things have become new* (2 Corinthians 5:17).

To this effect, born-again Christian believers become new persons in Christ from the instant Jesus Christ is received as Lord and Savior. A decision to serve the Lord offers you an opportunity to live your life as He did, making you a follower of Christ. Along with the benefits of your new status, there are also expectations or responsibilities attached to what becomes a "calling," as defined in the Bible. You become a disciple, ambassador, evangelist, with a ministry of reconciliation. Also mentioned in the Bible are enemies with the intent to hinder completion of your divine assignments, but you receive overriding supernatural ability to overcome such enemies. Jesus made clear to His followers there would be distractions, but they were to *"receive power when the Holy Spirit has come upon you"* (Acts 1:8a).

The blood of Jesus has set you free from accusations of satan who is the accuser of the brethren, which means that he reminds you of past failures and challenges you with wrongdoings of your ancestors. And satan continues to lie in order to work against you. However, the truth about your new life in Christ has been laid out clearly in the Word of God, and understanding of this truth is easily received as a matter of course for those in relationship with the Lord. Revelation is prerequisite to moving forward out of situations that are seemingly stagnant, and the indwelling presence of the Holy Spirit in your life arms you with authority to sever links with unrighteousness in your past and present experiences. The present-day warfare is centered on dismantling demonic structures aimed at Christian believers.

I consider life in habitual sin an insult on the blood of Jesus. My view may be considered insensitive, but it is quite the contrary. I personally believe when the body of believers fails to call in benefits of the divine sacrifice of Christ's blood, chiefly redemption from sin, we reject grace. Thus, a new mind-set is necessary if believers are to overcome evil of the day. Moreover, divine favor and blessings of financial increase are pronounced, including a promise of prophetic unction in Job 22:28a: *"You will also declare a thing, and it shall be established for you."*

It is important to remind ourselves that Job's words in Job22:28 were spoken before Calvary, but the fact is that the blood of Jesus has made us heirs and heiresses of greater favor and authority than Job foretold. The believer's authority is in the blood of Jesus and the Word of God.

Pray...

- Thank You, Lord, for my authority as a new creation believer.
- Thank You, Lord, for old things around me have passed away, and now my life has been made new in Your blood (see 2 Cor. 5:17).

The Weapon of the Believer's Authority

- Thank You, Lord, that in Your blood I am free from condemnation and past wrongdoing (see Rom. 8:1-2).
- Thank You that Your blood has given me a secure future, and as such, I shall stand in the righteousness of Christ to challenge enemies of my destiny (see Col. 1:14-15).
- Thank You, Lord, that I have been called, justified, and glorified to serve You. So now I can stand in Your righteousness to wait for my vindication (see Rom. 8:29-30; Job 14:14).

Recognizing Your Authority, Pray...

- Thank You, Lord, that You have trained my hands for war and my fingers for battle (see Ps. 144:1).
- Thank You, Lord, that I am Your battle axe and Your weapon of war (see Jer. 50:9).
- Thank You, Lord, that the spiritual ammunition with which I defeat the enemies of my destiny shall be like those of an expert warrior; none shall return in vain (see Jer. 50:9).
- Thank You, Lord, that You are my strength. You will make my feet like deer's feet, and You will make me walk on my high places above evil (see Hab. 3:19).
- Thank You, Lord, that every battle raging around my life belongs to You (see 2 Chron. 20:15).
- I trust in Your saving grace, Lord, as I shall see the wicked snared in his own hands (see Ps. 9:16).

Confess...

I now renounce and denounce any hidden sin and other compromise in my life that may hinder my prayers. *"Create in me a clean heart, O God, and renew a steadfast spirit within me. Do not cast me away from Your presence, and do not take Your Holy Spirit from me. Restore to me the joy of Your salvation, and uphold me by Your generous Spirit. Then I will teach transgressors Your ways, and sinners shall be converted to You"* (Ps. 51:10-13).

PRAYER SECTION 7

The Weapon of His Name

But thanks be to God, who gives us the victory through our Lord Jesus Christ (1 Corinthians 15:57).

The name of Jesus is another potent weapon of spiritual warfare. I sincerely believe the mention of the Lord's name invokes His presence and power, for the Bible emphasizes the power in the name of Jesus:

...for there is no other name under Heaven given among men by which we must be saved (Acts 4:12).

The Authority of His Name

Calling on the name of Jesus moves Heaven on behalf of the caller. Jesus Himself taught, "*And whatever you ask in My name, that I will do, that the Father may be glorified in the Son. If you ask anything in My name, I will do it*" (John 14:13-14). I particularly enjoy praying with and also in the name of Jesus. It gives me a wonderful sense of confidence and security.

The Weapon of His Name

Prayer simply means communication with God. An important rule of communication demands response from a person addressed by another in voluntary conversation, and a natural and reasonable expectation is to anticipate response from someone you are conversing with. You do not expect to be ignored in those circumstances, which would be considered rude or impolite. Likewise, when speaking to God as a child, you should expect Him to respond (see Mark 9:23-24; 11:24).

God desires to hear your voice calling to Him, not only in need, but in a relationship of intimacy and boldness (see Jer. 33:3). So, when you use the name of Jesus in spiritual warfare, as a person who is familiar with its power, your prayer language immediately adopts a sound of confidence. Moreover, at the mention of the name of Jesus, every knee will someday bow and every tongue will confess Him as Lord (see Phil. 2:9-11). The Bible is clear on the authority commanded by the name of Jesus—a name by which both believers and non-believers shall be judged.

As a person who loves to pray, I am reminded of the authority I come under when I pray the name of the Lord Jesus. Furthermore, when addressing a person in conversation, it is common courtesy to use their name. Likewise, when you pray, declare the name of Jesus over any situation you seek to present before the Lord.

His Name Destroys the Works of the Devil

I must point out that spiritual warfare is not all about aggressive speech, as some tend to believe and practice, but both praise and silence are powerful weapons of warfare (see Josh. 6:10). At times, my most effective times of engaging in spiritual warfare have been when I've praised the Lord over circumstances and situations. Often, after thanking the Lord for His shed blood, I will usually, although not in any particular order or regime, begin to lift up the name of Jesus—a form of praise. Lifting up the name of Jesus Christ in a sense disengages evil spirits working through humans to perpetrate wickedness (see John 12:32). When you pray in the name of Jesus, a message of commitment to a name given that is higher than any other name is released (see Phil. 2:9). Demons flee at the mention of the name of Jesus

Christ. Satan fully understands your mission as a child of the Lord. I often remind satan of a truth he dreads: *"For this purpose the Son of God was manifested, that He might destroy the works of the devil"* (1 John 3:8b). I then hold onto the name of Jesus through the thoughts of my heart, reminding whatever situation that is causing warfare that I have also been manifested *"to destroy the works of the devil."* Once your heart's desire is honorable in God, the Holy Spirit will assist you by giving fresh language with which to call on the name of Jesus.

In the case of the seven sons of Sceva, the demon spirit, which attacked the men, feared the name of Jesus. The demon spirit was also terrified of the apostolic authority with which Paul's ministry was conducted. Consequently, when the sons sought to clone Paul's spiritual authority, they received a beating (see Acts 19:13-17). No demon can challenge a person who understands authority in the name of Jesus unless such a person is not under spiritual authority himself. The Bible emphasizes the importance of the name of Jesus through several Scriptures. Jesus Himself said His Father would do "anything" asked in His name, and eventually, His disciples would cast out demons in His name (see Acts 16:16-18).

Spiritual authority is released when we use the wonderfully powerful name of Jesus who was manifested to destroy every work of the devil. Spiritual wars against satan's followers would have been unimaginable if Jesus had not defeated lucifer with His blood (see Col. 2:14-15). I have included some Scriptures to remind you of the powerful name of Jesus as you engage in warfare to break bonds of wickedness in your life.

- Jesus said, *"...whatever you ask the Father in My name He may give you"* (John 15:16b).
- Proverbs cautions, *"The name of the Lord is a strong tower"* (Prov. 18:10a).
- *"And whatever you ask in My name, that I will do, that the Father may be glorified in the Son. If you ask anything in My name, I will do it"* (John 14:13-14).

- *"For this purpose the Son of God was manifested, that He might destroy the works of the devil"* (1 John 3:8b).
- *"In My name they will cast out demons; they will speak with new tongues"* (Mark 16:17b).
- *"And the name of the Lord Jesus was magnified"* (Acts 19:17b).

Pray...

- Lord, I thank You for Your wonderful name. I thank You, Lord, for Your name which is a strong tower providing shelter for Your children in times of need. I do pray, Lord, "Teach me to know You and to use Your name as a weapon of protection against the devil's siege."
- I raise Your name, Jesus, as a banner over my life, my family, and my relationships.
- In Your name, Jesus, I bring my anxieties, cares, confusion, sickness, worries, [present your case] before You, Lord.
- In Your name, Lord, I address any spirits behind the situation in my life, and I command them to bow to the lordship of Jesus Christ, Amen.
- In Your name, Lord, I call for every bond of wickedness around, over, and in my life to be exposed.
- In Your name, Lord, I ask for courage to break bonds of wickedness and other soul ties in my life.

It is important to bear in mind that all negative circumstances and situations are not necessarily due to demonic manipulations. Overextension of spiritual authority could expose you to demonic warfare as seen in the case of the seven sons of Sceva (see Acts 19:13-16). Prayer is a humble sacrifice offered to the Lord, so it will be useful at this point to ask the Lord to reveal compromises or other bonds of wickedness in your life that should be brought under subjection to the lordship of Jesus (see 2 Cor. 10:5).

PRAYER SECTION 8

Break the Power of Fear

Fear is an end-time principality, threatening lives of many in the present days. Fear is not of God and should be rejected as you say these prayers. *"God has not given us a spirit of fear, but of power and of love and of a sound mind"* (2 Tim. 1:7).

The devil attacks believers using fear as one of his main weapons. The Lord spoke to me a few years ago and told me to study fear-related illnesses in the United Kingdom. I was amazed by the statistics and amount of revenue channelled toward alleviating problems caused by mental health issues. Fear is a foul spirit that must be cast away from your life with love. The Bible reminds us, *"There is no fear in love; but perfect love casts out fear, because fear involves torment"* (1 John 4:18a).

Jesus died to free you from torment. His love for you is perfect, undemanding, and all-encompassing, and it will break bonds of wickedness in your life so that you can walk in total freedom from torment.

The apostle Paul charged his spiritual son, Timothy, to *"wage the good warfare"* according to the prophecies made previously concerning him (see 1 Tim. 1:18b). Timothy was also admonished to *"Stir up the gift"* inside of him (see 1 Tim. 2:6). Timothy himself was facing challenges from false doctrine taught by his detractors, and he probably faced intimidation, a form of fear from his challengers. His spiritual father implored him to wage "the good warfare" with the word of faith. Spiritual warfare is a reality, not a figment of man's imagination; and spiritual wars are won not with natural weapons, such as retaliatory actions but with divinely revealed weapons such as praise, silence, and others outlined in this book. Sadly, some people deride aspects of spiritual warfare because of unfamiliar knowledge or where the mind has yet to receive full understanding. However, it is unwise to dismiss perspectives or spiritual insight simply for the sake of familiar or safe understanding. The Bible warns, "*We know in part and we prophesy in part*" (1 Cor. 13:9). God's Word is prophecy, and as I mentioned earlier, it is also an effective weapon of war with which the good warfare is waged and won (see 1 Tim. 1:18). Our warfare is good because Jesus has already defeated our enemy (see Col. 2:14-15).

Fear is an enemy of Christian believers—an enemy that must be defeated. No matter how incapable you feel or inadequately disposed to the spiritual battles around you, it is important to remember Jesus Christ is strong when you are weak, and He promises, "*My grace is sufficient for you, for My strength is made perfect in weakness*" (2 Cor. 12:9a).

So you must arise and take authority over every ploy of the devil to hinder your purpose. The message of this book implores readers to purposefully confront demonic activities around their lives. And in readiness for inevitable spiritual contentions, you also need to adopt a lifestyle of transparency—another great weapon of spiritual warfare. Fear stands as a major threat to advancing the Kingdom of God—a threat that needs to be destroyed.

Declare...

- I break and destroy every stronghold of fear over my life, in Jesus' name.
- I break and destroy every manifestation of fear around my life, in Jesus' name.
- I break and destroy every cycle of fear operating around my life, in Jesus' name.
- I break and destroy every agent of fear at work against my destiny, in Jesus' name.
- I break and destroy fear-releasing spirits hindering my destiny, in Jesus' name.
- I break and destroy every demonic covenant fanning the flame of fear against my life, in Jesus' name.
- I break and destroy every spiritual door through which spirits of fear are accessing my life, in Jesus' name.
- I break and destroy every unrighteous foundation in my life that has tolerated the spirits of fear, in Jesus' name.
- I break and destroy every demonic covenant operating in my life, which has strengthened the spirits of fear now working against my purpose, in Jesus' name.
- I break and destroy every identity with which the spirits of fear (stress, anxiety) are attacking my life, in Jesus' name.
- I unmask the spirits of fear and demand their identities to be exposed at my word, in Jesus' name.

Press Into Breakthrough...

- I thank You, Lord, for answering my prayers (see Jer. 33:3).
- I shall now walk in freedom and power of Your blood to fulfill my destiny (see Rom. 8:1).
- I shall not be afraid of the terror by night; and I shall not be afraid of the arrow that flies by the day, for the Lord is with me (see Ps. 91:5-6).

- I thank You, Lord, for Your Word assures me: "*The nations have sunk down in the pit which they made; in the net which they hid, their own foot is caught*" (Ps. 9:15).
- I thank You, Lord, for Your Word assures me, "*The wicked is snared in the work of his own hands,*" so I shall not fear (Ps. 9:16).
- I thank You, Lord, for the "*wickedness of the wicked*" has come to an end over my life (see Ps. 7:9).
- I thank You, Lord, as I now enter into Your rest.

In Jesus' name I have prayed, Amen.

PRAYER SECTION 9

Establish Boundaries

Every prayer section in this book is to be considered a step toward your preparation as a dangerous prayer warrior. Praying these prayers places your life in the spotlight, as you break bonds of wickedness in your own life and then minister true freedom to others.

The psalmist prayed humbly, *"Lead me, O Lord, in Your righteousness because of my enemies"* (Ps. 5:8a). David was speaking of literal enemies, whereas when we refer to enemies, we are talking about manifestations of evil or demonic activities and the spirits behind such. Unfortunately, evil spirits operate through humans as well as circumstances, but when engaging in warfare to dislodge the enemy, your focus should always be on spiritual dynamics. Otherwise, you may pray against humans instead of spirits.

Boundaries of Righteousness

The psalmist saw the need to walk in the righteousness of God in order to invoke God's power and protection. As a matter of fact, he

Establish Boundaries

recognized God's ability to defend in Psalm 5:11a, which says, *"But let all those rejoice who put their trust in You; let them ever shout for joy, because **You defend them**"* (emphasis added). However, God cannot defend us if sin is present in our lives, because sin separates us from God, whether it is clear-cut sin, or a "weight" as recorded in Hebrews 12:1, or "secret faults" as the psalmist mentions (see Ps. 19:2). Therefore, it is important to establish strong boundaries of righteousness around your life so that your lifestyle is driven by the Spirit of excellence, which is of our holy God.

I remember so clearly at a point during 2005 when the Lord gave me a promise from Isaiah 52:1b, which says, *"For the uncircumcised and the unclean shall no longer come to you."* As I began to meditate on this Scripture in light of the New Testament meaning of circumcision, which is now of the heart, I received understanding of my promise. In effect, the Lord was promising to protect me from people whose hearts were not within godly boundaries of imputed righteousness. I was not perfect, but the Lord was ensuring I did not enter into bonds of wickedness capable of giving the enemy foothold into my life. The Lord set a boundary over my life which I needed to maintain. Psalm 125:3a confirms the issue of boundaries with the Lord's charge, which holds: *"For the scepter of wickedness shall not rest on the land **allotted** to the righteous"* (emphasis added).

Boundaries of Protection

Your personal life and personal belongings are blessings resulting from God's manifold grace on your life, and you should protect God's blessings from satan who is a thief. But bear in mind that without the Lord's assistance, human safeguards fail (see Ps. 127:1). Through carelessness, ignorance, and all sorts of other reasons, believers may give the devil options or open doors through which he can strike. For instance, a person who receives prayers to break a stronghold of homosexuality needs to receive practical help in lifestyle reorientation. Simply attending periodic cell group meetings might not suffice when demon spirits behind unrighteous urges attack. Additional practical assistance may translate into spiritual boundary lines around their new life and choice. Such practical steps serve as notice to the devil that a new life has begun, whereas the devil thrives in vacuums when gaps tend to exist.

The Bible recognizes the devil's agenda to seek reentry into any foundation, ground, or vacuum left through carelessness of some sort. In fact, the devil can return with seven more wicked demons (see Matt. 12:43-45). *Seven* is the number for completion and perfection. The devil is often seeking to perfect his evil acts and to bring completion to his agenda. It is for this reason satan deploys every device at his disposal against unsuspecting victims.

Yet God sets boundaries today, even as He set a boundary for the spirit of death in the judgment of Egypt. God is a God of order. He found it necessary to set a boundary of protection around His people although He was the initiator of that particular judgment against Egypt. He said, *"Now the blood shall be a sign for you on the houses where you are. And when I see the blood, I will pass over you; and the plague shall not be on you to destroy you when I strike the land of Egypt"* (Exod. 12:13).

By establishing boundaries around your life, you are, in effect, declaring that whatever spirits are bound will not gain re-entry into your life or any person's life for whom you stand in intercession.

Boundaries of Evil

At this point, in your prayers, it would be pertinent to address with boldness and in truth any compromise or sin in your life. Only then can the issue of existing or known compromises in family lines be addressed. The devil also sets boundaries, carefully watching for sin that places a believer inside his boundary lines. I have interacted with many faithful intercessors who have struggled with cases of generation line poverty. Despite their faithfulness in prayer and service to the Lord, I have watched friends suffer from lack over the years. As these incidences troubled my soul, I began praying for understanding. How could faithful men and women receive words of promise from God's Word yet still be so aggressively challenged with apparent failure? I was

Establish Boundaries

amazed by the understanding I received. Unless faithful believers set boundaries around their lives by operating in mind-sets of freedom, spirits holding entire family lines ransom may also attack them. These are the spirits challenging spiritual harvests from covenant promises to the Church, just as Israel experienced in the hands of the Midianites in the days of Gideon (see Judges 6:3).

Declare...

- Lord, I thank You for Your blood shed at Calvary for me.
- I now draw a blood line around my life, my family, and other relationships.
- I bring my life under submission to Your divine rule and to natural, ordained, spiritual authority (e.g, your pastor or other Christian mentors).
- I call upon You, the God of Israel, who neither slumbers nor sleeps, to watch over my life.
- I call upon You, Holy Spirit, to keep me within boundaries of truth.
- I call upon Your angels to encamp around my life.
- I call upon You, Lord, to anoint watchmen and intercessors over my life with fresh oil to present me before You.
- I call upon You, Lord, to preserve me in the boundaries of Your blood, Your Word, Your name, and Your authority in my life.
- I thank You, Lord, for answering my calls according to Jeremiah 33:3. In Jesus' name, Amen.

Legislate in Accordance With Job 22:28...

- Every foul spirit from the past now challenging my destiny must now remain silent in Jesus' name.
- Every voice of familiar spirits, or voice of the dead speaking to any living persons, such as psychics, concerning my life and my family line must now remain silent in Jesus' name.

- Every voice of opposition counteracting God's plans for my life must be denied access in the realms of the spirit and influence upon the earth.
- Every familiar voice from my past arming my present disposition of information with which to attack my future must now be destroyed.
- Every word spoken or written, and every action or omission now compromising my future is nullified by the blood of Jesus.
- I command every spirit being, which is being used by satan to challenge my future, to surrender at the name of Jesus; I declare that you have been bound and cast into hell at my word, and so shall it be (see Job 22:28).

Amen.

Now Declare to the Enemy...

- You shall not *multiply* your works.
- You shall not *metamorphose* your works.
- You shall not *redistribute* your works.
- You shall not *recreate* your works.
- You shall not *reinstate* your works.
- You shall not *reinvent* your works.
- You shall not *reincarnate* your works.
- You shall not *repackage* your works.
- You shall not *regenerate* your works.
- You shall not *resurrect* your works.
- You shall not *revamp* your works.

As I have decreed your end in Jesus' name, so shall it be. Amen.

When you pray, it is important to seal every prayer with potent declaration according to the Word of God (see Ps. 119:89). Elijah, a man of prayer, declared a drought over Israel for three and a half

Establish Boundaries

years at His word (see 1 Kings 17:1). The Lord then honored Elijah's faith and prayers, and his ministry was subsequently recognized and honored in the New Testament as well: *"The effective, fervent prayer of a righteous man avails much"* (James 5:16).

STRENGTHEN YOUR PRAYERS

Assuredly, I say to you, whatever you bind on earth will be bound in heaven, and whatever you loose on earth will be loosed in heaven. Again I say to you that if two of you agree on earth concerning anything that they ask, it will be done for them by My Father in heaven (Matthew 18:18-19).

When confronting evil foundations, it is important to be circumspect, especially as the Bible warns us of the evil day (see Eph. 5:16-18). The Holy Spirit is our wonderful teacher who guides us to the truth, and I, personally, remain a grateful student of the Lord's school of prayer (see Luke 11:1). The Lord has given me a language of expression, which I then pray back to Him with confidence (see Rom. 8:26-27). A lot of believers, especially those in the Western world, struggle with apostolic language necessary for certain levels of spiritual warfare. Prayers at the level I refer to are termed "violent prayers" by some in apostolic communities and are included in this book to provoke you to prepare for inevitable warfare of an evil day. In addition, you must arm yourself with radical holiness in order to function in covenant promise of protection from the wiles of the enemy (see Isa. 54:17), for unless fundamental wrongs in your life are placed at the altar of sacrifice, doors of accusation will remain open to the devil.

Pray...

I stand on the Word of God, and I declare:

- My prayers shall not be *resisted* by the devil and his cohorts, in Jesus' name (see Job 22:28).
- My prayers shall not be *challenged* by diviners, sorcerers, witches, wizards, or any other occultism coalition, in Jesus' name (see Isa. 44:25).

- My prayers shall not be *sabotaged* by the devil working through humans. No human agents or other agents such as birds, cats, or airs of oppression will be used to sabotage my declarations, in Jesus' name.
- My prayers shall not be *derailed* by my carelessness, sin, or any other form of compromise in my life, in Jesus' name (see Heb. 11:6).
- My prayers shall not be *hindered* by any covenants, agreements, or other pacts I have made with evil men and women who operate in disguises, in Jesus' name.
- My prayers shall not be *shipwrecked* by my lack of faith, apathy, compromise, doubt, or any other condition in disagreement with the Word of God for my life, in Jesus' name.
- My prayers shall not be *undermined* by discouragers, slanderers, gossips, or any other form of negative speech, or actions of men, in Jesus' name.
- My prayers shall not be *nullified* by my unbelief, negative words, or another's unbelief and negative words; but my prayers shall yield me bountiful harvests, in Jesus' name.
- My prayers shall not be subverted by demonic troops or other agents I have failed to massacre with the Word of God.

Amen.

PRAYER SECTION 10

Set Yourself Free

EXAMINE YOUR LIFE

As I mentioned previously, the devil is incapable of derailing divine purposes of God in the life of a righteous believer. Consider Noah's life. His righteousness was remembered by God in a time of judgment. Whereas, sin opens the door to satan's domain and rule. The Bible warns that the wages of sin is death, and a Christian life lived outside the presence of God is likened to death.

Therefore, in order to prepare your life as a true disciple of Christ and a carrier of divine purposes, it is important to seek the Lord so that He may reveal hidden sin or any secret fault. The psalmist confessed to hiding the Word of God in his heart so that he would not sin against God (see Ps. 119:11).

To prepare for the epic spiritual wars of our time, believers are to confront sin, rebellion, and other forms of unrighteousness in our lives. The way to win is the way of holiness.

I Stand on Your Word in Psalm 1, and I Decree Over My Life...

- I shall not walk in the counsel of the ungodly, nor stand in the path of sinners, nor sit in the seat of the scornful, for Your name's sake, O Lord.
- I shall delight and meditate in Your Word day and night.
- I shall be like a tree planted by the rivers of water that brings forth its fruit in its season; my leaf shall not wither.
- I shall prosper in whatever I do. Amen.

I Stand on Your Word in Psalm 51, and I Decree Over My Life...

- I pray, create in me a clean heart, O God; renew a steadfast spirit within me.

I Stand on Your Word in Psalm 24, and I Decree Over My Life...

- I shall not lift up my soul to an idol, nor shall I swear deceitfully.

I Stand on Your Word in Psalm 15, and I Decree Over My Life...

- I shall not backbite with my tongue.
- I shall not do evil to my neighbor, nor will I take up reproach against my friend.
- I shall honor those who fear the Lord.
- I shall stand my ground and wait on the Lord.
- I shall not put out my money to usury.
- I shall not take a bribe against the innocent, for God is with me.

Therefore...

- I renounce every demonic covenant, agreement, pact, treaty, contract, or any other ties *I have entered* into knowingly or unknowingly, directly or indirectly, with ungodly men and women through:

    1. Associations.
    2. Friendships.

3. Business.

   4. Employment.

   5. Sexual contact.

   6. Food.

   7. Drink.

   In Jesus' name, Amen.

- I renounce and denounce every demonic covenant, agreement, pact, treaty, contract, or any other ties *entered into* on my behalf by any person in my:

   1. Family line.

   2. Ancestry.

   3. Generations.

   4. Business links.

   5. Trade links.

   6. Marriage.

   7. Friendships.

   8. Any other relationships.

   In Jesus' name, Amen.

Now Pray...

- I renounce and denounce every *unholy alliance I have bonded* myself to knowingly or unknowingly, directly or indirectly. In Jesus' name, Amen.

- I renounce and denounce every *unholy alliance I have been bonded to* knowingly or unknowingly, directly or indirectly. In Jesus' name, Amen.

- I renounce and denounce any *agreements I have entered into* unknowingly in my sleep with demonic forces through:

   1. Eating in dreams.

   2. Familiar spirits.

3. Spirit husband.

4. Spirit wife.

5. Spirit friends.

In Jesus' name, Amen.

- I renounce and denounce *generation covenants*, agreements, pacts, treaties, contracts, or any other ties *I have bonded* myself to knowingly or unknowingly, directly or indirectly, in Jesus' name.

- I renounce and denounce generational covenants, agreements, pacts, treaties, contracts, or any other ties *I have been bonded to*.

I decree over my life that the blood of Jesus has delivered me from every requirement of evil agreements that was against my life (see Col. 2:14); and now *I walk free* of demands of the devil on my life, including sickness, poverty, divorce, unemployment, and barrenness.

I Declare Over My Life...

- The power of evil agreements working against me are now destroyed in Jesus' name.

- The power of evil spells spoken against me are now destroyed in Jesus' name.

- The power of curses and covenants speaking down my family line are now nullified in Jesus' name.

- The power of destiny-robbing spirits operating against my life are destroyed in Jesus' name.

- The power of identity-stealing demons unleashed against me are destroyed in Jesus' name.

- The power of cloning spirits copying my spiritual gifts are now destroyed.

- I shall walk in my freedom in Christ Jesus to fulfill His purpose in me. Amen.

SET YOURSELF FREE

God is a holy God, and those who are called to serve and worship Him are also required to live holy lives. Therefore, it is important to confess and renounce the sin in your life that serves as an open door for the enemy to attack a believer in Christ Jesus.

> *But as He who called you is holy, you also be holy in all your conduct, because it is written, "Be holy, for I am holy"* (1 Peter 1:15).

The "Weight" That Ensnares

Some in the Body of Christ delude themselves when they assume that some sins are of a lesser degree than others. For instance, they might believe that exaggeration is not as serious a sin as outright lying. But sin is sin; and no matter how much sin is dressed up, it leads to death. Furthermore, a believer who allows sin in his or her life is vulnerable to demonic spirits seeking new homes. When invisible spirits are permitted to dwell in persons in our thoughts, such spirits receive authority to multiply. On the other hand, God wants us to live free of spiritual encumbrances and enjoy full freedom received through the blood of Jesus.

The writer of Hebrews urges believers to lay aside the "sin" and "weight" that so easily besets us (see Heb. 12:1-2). Sin appears to be easily recognized by mature Christians, but perhaps not so readily for younger ones. Apart from the obvious wrongs, the Bible encourages that we also consider the "weight" that so easily ensnares the children of God. The devil understands his end is at hand; hence, he has heightened his attack on believers (see Rev. 12:12), and he carries out his evil manipulations using every device imaginable. He deceives hearts by inciting attitudes that offend God, as was in the case of King Saul (see 1 Sam. 15). In his typical chameleon nature, the devil changes color to become an accuser of the same saints he has deceived in the first place.

The time has come for the Body of Christ to manifest the power of the Kingdom of Heaven (see 1 Cor. 2:4). The authority of a believer in sin is, however, easily challenged. Their compromised hearts are exposed by the devil responsible for deceiving people into sin in the first place. Unrighteous foundations in the Church as a whole and lives of individual believers need to be spiritually excavated now so that residing sin is dealt with. Such lives can only then be rebuilt as houses of praise—a symbol of the tabernacle of David (see Amos 9:11). The time has come to silence the accuser of the brethren who continues to challenge righteousness in the lives of believers.

Unlawful Spiritual Contracts

In order to advance into the realm of the supernatural it is important to seize the moment by receiving revelation of bonds of wickedness in your life. The next line of action is to *break* unrighteous covenants through violent prayer as I have prepared for you in this book.

Covenant means agreement or a contract between two parties. *Contracts* confer rights and impose obligations. Unrighteous agreements or covenants entered into, albeit innocently by a believer or someone else on behalf of a believer, can have far-reaching consequences. As mentioned, such agreements confer rights and impose obligations. The prayers in this section are aimed at arming you with revelation of consequences of demonic spiritual ties and the significance of having them broken and destroyed in Jesus' name.

It is extremely important to bear in mind that covenants, soul ties, or other forms of bondage that have been broken over your life will seek re-entry. Such spirits will take advantage of any open doors or spiritual doors reopened through subsequent sinning; hence, it is important to establish boundaries as directed in Prayer Section 9 (see "Establish Boundaries").

Do Not Negotiate With the Enemy

Demonic agreements and soul ties give the enemy impetus to demand the right to strike people with conditions such as sickness and poverty. However, the blood of Jesus offers a new way to every child of God, yet so many are still encumbered by obligations from their past, which compromise their future. The time has come to cut soul ties that give the enemy access into your life.

In the story of Samson, the Philistines symbolized towering, persistent problems that continue today to plague the lives of so many well-meaning believers. Samson destroyed his enemies, the Philistines, after he broke his soul tie with Delilah. Only then did his hair, symbolizing spiritual authority, start to grow back. When you strive for your deliverance from unrighteous spiritual agreements, your spiritual authority will increase as well.

As you pray the prayers in this book by faith, you shall receive supernatural strength to slay more Philistines than you can ever imagine, as Samson did when he brought down the temple. You have been tested in the furnace of afflictions so that you can become a fortified city and a house of refuge (see Jer. 1:18).

Pray...

Lord, You have tested my heart; You have visited me in the night; You have tried me and have found nothing; I have purposed that my mouth shall not transgress. Concerning the works of men, by the word of Your lips, I have kept away from the paths of the destroyer. Uphold my steps in Your paths, that my footsteps may not slip. I have called upon You, for You will hear me, O God; incline Your ear to me, and hear my speech. Show Your marvelous lovingkindness by Your right hand, O You who save those who trust in You from those who rise up against them. Keep me as the apple of Your eye; hide me under the shadow of Your wings, from the wicked who oppress me, from my deadly enemies who surround me [in Jesus' name, Amen] (Psalm 17:3-9).

PRAYER SECTION 11

Disarm the Enemy

APPLYING PRESSURE ON HELL

For This Purpose You Were Made Manifest

The devil is a liar who operates in all sorts of disguises to carry out his evil plans. The most dangerous mistake any believer can make is to assume the devil does not exist, or that he is a friend of the Church who needs ministry. It is true that satan's works were destroyed at Calvary, but it is still up to believers to appropriate the gains of the blood of Jesus.

The Son of man was made manifest to destroy the works of the devil; and as a child of the living God, you also were made manifest for the same reason—to destroy the works of the devil. As satan continues to war against the advancement of God's Kingdom on earth, operating through a variety of disguises and aliases, we are to apply our authority in Christ to discern and expose his disguises. Our common goal should be to destroy the works of the devil.

Disarm the Enemy

I Declare According To Your Word in Micah 4:13...

- I shall arise and thresh evil plans of the enemy, as Your Word commands me.
- Thank You, Lord, for You have made my horn (strength) iron; and You have made my hooves bronze; and so I shall beat in pieces many peoples.
- By Your blood I shall plunder them and consecrate their gain to the Lord, and their substance I shall deliver to You, Lord, of the whole earth, in Jesus' name.

Lord, I Pray...

- That Your light will shine over all the earth to expose channels of evil that war against my purpose, in Jesus' name (see Heb. 4:13).
- There is no creature hidden from Your sight, but all things are naked and open to Your eyes; for it is You that all men must make account (see Heb. 4:13).
- That the lamp of the wicked shall be put off as You have said in Your Word in Proverbs.

Thank You, Lord, for Your Word in Isaiah 40—I Apply the Power of Your Word and Declare...

- May there not be any hiding place for evil forces that war against my destiny.
- May mountains bow down to expose them.
- May valleys rise to spew them out.
- May hills bend to throw them out.
- May narrow paths be straightened to expose their deeds.
- May the earth shake under their feet so that their devices fail to take effect.
- May the land give them up into my righteous hands.

In Jesus' name, Amen!

WEAKEN THEIR POWER BASE

It is interesting to note that satan uses isolation to attack his victims, but his forces do not work in isolation. I remember several years ago when the Spirit of the Lord took me in the spirit to overlook the deployment section in hell. We watched as lucifer stood on a busy warehouse floor while his hit men shifted demonic assignments in white envelopes. We watched as he called up his demonic task force. Surprisingly, they came in twos, threes, and fours, but never alone. Each group was handed an envelope with a single instruction—"Shut them down!" Satan was referring to the nature of havoc these invisible spirit beings would cause on the earth. Although every difficult circumstance in your life is not a result of demonic influence, a good number of unexplainable situations and circumstances are rooted in demonic manipulations.

I then saw the manager of a multi-complex building that my ministry was renting at the time. I had my reservations in the past about the lady but was never really sure if my perception could be defined as spiritual discernment or mere suspicion. She appeared before lucifer with a company of two. The Holy Spirit and I watched as she was given a white envelope with the same instruction, "Shut them down!"

I shared my experience with close intercessors and then organized an emergency prayer meeting to stand in the gap for those who would be affected by the contents of every white envelope given out. Amazingly, the manager approached me a few days later asking for a lease renewal. Equally bizarre was the fact that she admitted that our office lease was not up for renewal for another three months but she needed it done then.

I realized the Lord had enabled me to witness satanic dispatching for a reason, and now I was witnessing the reality of what I thought was only a supernatural spiritual experience. I was being confronted in the natural by a spirit working through the manager whom I had seen accepting an envelope with the instruction, "Shut them down." With benefit of spiritual maturity, I now understand that the personality I saw receiving her satanic dispatch letter was a familiar spirit attached to our manager at the time. The spirit responsible for some of her unexplainable behavior was being dispatched to her to incite her against our organization. It is spirit beings such as I have described that engineer and ferment strife even in bloodlines. The time has come to evict illegal spiritual occupants of our family lines.

Lord...

- I release confusion against the convergence of evil warring against my destiny, in Jesus' name, and by the power of the blood of Jesus (see 2 Chron. 20).
- I release angelic delegates to scatter their evil alliance, in Jesus' name.
- I release praise and worship in the spiritual climate over my nation, city, street, and home, to pierce every dark cloud formation with the marvelous light of Jesus Christ.
- I release the power of the blood of Jesus against the foundation of their gatherings. May their foundation cave in, to swallow their rebellion, as it was in the days of Korah (see Num. 16).
- I release the power of the blood of Jesus to arrest them. May they surrender to the saving power of Jesus Christ.
- I release the Word of God to break their power base into pieces, in Jesus' name.

I Declare to the Demonic Coalition Coming Against Me and My Family in Accordance With Isaiah 8:9-10...

- Be shattered, O you peoples, and be broken in pieces!
- Give ear, all you from satanism, occultism, new age, covens, and citadels of the devil in the east, west, north, and south of [name your immediate surrounding].
- Gird yourselves, but be broken in pieces.
- Take counsel together, but it will come to nothing.
- Speak the word, but it will not stand, for God is with me.

Lord, in Accordance With Your Word in Isaiah 29:3, I Pray...

- Encamp against evil forces that are operating against my destiny.
- Encamp against evil encampments that plot against me, like a mound.
- Lay siege against them like a mound.
- Raise siege works against them.
- Bring them down in their plots.
- May their speech concerning my future and destiny be made low and not take effect.
- May their words, their voices be like mediums—powerless—out of the ground (see Isa. 29:4).

In Jesus' name.

PRAYER SECTION 12

Defeat the Enemy

BIND THE ENEMY

When Peter spoke the identity of Jesus Christ by revelation, the Lord honored him for pressing into his Father for a revelation of whom Christ is (see Matt. 16:7). Jesus Christ in return revealed Peter's identity as a key building rock that would be established on Jesus.

A life that is built on revelation of Christ's authority can never be prevailed against by the gates of hades (see Matt. 16:18) A believer armed with insight will know to receive the keys to the Kingdom of Heaven and to use its authority purposefully. Jesus taught, *"Whatever you bind on earth will be bound in heaven, and whatever you loose on earth will be loosed in heaven"* (Matt. 16:19b).

The Church is under siege from multicultural demon spirits who understand the universal language of faith; however, apostolic warriors should be able to effectively legislate the mind of Christ over spiritual wickedness in heavenly places. Spiritual wars are not to be fought with natural weapons such as emotional speech, human judgments, or spears and arrows. Defeating the wickedness of our present time will necessitate focused strategic level spiritual warfare.

Declare...

- Standing on the Word of God in Isaiah 54:17, *I decree* demonic weapons of the enemy *shall not prosper* over my life, in Jesus' name.

- Standing on the Word of God in Colossians 2:14, *I decree*, that every soul tie and other demonic bonding, compromising my faith and life, have been nullified—*never to take effect*, in Jesus' name.

- Standing on the Word of God in Matthew 18:18, *I decree* that every demonic alliance, or association, bound on earth from operating against my life *are also bound in Heaven*, in Jesus' name.

- Standing on the Word of God in Deuteronomy 28:7, *I declare*, when the enemy comes in one direction, he will flee in seven different ways, in Jesus' name.

- Standing on the Word of God in Joshua 5:9, *I decree* the reproach of Egypt has been rolled away from my life, *so I shall not suffer from demonic oppression*, in Jesus' name.

- Standing on the Word of God in Exodus 14:13, *I declare* that the Egyptian I see today, I shall see again no more, forever, in Jesus' name. *Therefore, every difficulty I have encountered shall no longer overpower me, as I have prayed*, in Jesus' name.

- Standing on the Word of God in Exodus 15:26, *I declare* that the diseases of the Egyptians shall not be my portion. *I therefore decree that I shall not suffer from incurable, contagious, infectious or any other type of disease*, in Jesus' name.

I decree that every demonic agent that contends over my destiny must surrender to the lordship of Jesus Christ.

Defeat the Enemy

Study Your Adversary...

- Demonic servicemen keep satan's structures functional.
- Demonic workmen serve satan's evil agendas.
- Demonic repairmen reconnect channels of distribution of satanic missiles.
- Demonic counsellors release deception and foolish counsel.
- Demonic caterers serve evil concoctions on demonic plates.

Every other satanic agent or spirit employed to keep satan's kingdom of darkness effective and functional against my life, my family, my nation, and my church are *destroyed* for my sake, in Jesus' name.

The Devil Is a Liar!

Satan is revealed in the Word of God as a murderer, thief, lawless, liar, deceiver, and an enemy (see John 10:10). He uses these disguises to attack and strike his fiery darts against his targets. Satanic fiery darts take advantage of openings, which have been made through personal and corporate sin, to accuse and encumber victims. Satan is the sneaky serpent who hides from exposure; he is a deceiver. He deceives God's people into believing a Christian or church-goer cannot be used to challenge the purposes of God in the lives of other believers. Satan and his demons hide as invisible spirits, controlling lives of believers from pulpits to pews; and with pride, he raises his victims up into superstars, and with ignominy, he fells them like the famous oak tree.

Satan enslaves minds of believers, seducing them into jealousy, competition, and rivalry. For example, a child of God who takes to lying is a slave to sin, and sin is of the devil (see Rom. 6:6). Such a person opens doors of his or her life to a demonic presence, not of flesh and blood, but of invisible spirits. It is important to use our ammunition of the Word of God, power in the blood of Jesus, and spiritual authority vested in believers in Christ Jesus to destroy the works of satan.

The Church is to engage in strategic level spiritual warfare to dislodge wicked evil spirits contending for hearts and souls of men on

streets in our communities. Our role is to pray for freedom of souls from demonic oppression (see Mark 16:17).

SHUT EVIL DOORS

A fact I have mentioned several times, which I believe is worthy of reiteration, is that satan is only able to effect his evil devices if access is given to him to enter into lives. Our God shuts doors that no man can open. However, sin, unholy alliances, demonic covenants, soul ties, and other unrighteous agreements entered into may serve as open doors into people's lives. And unless such entry points are identified and closed, the devil may establish repeated patterns of attack, using well-structured sequences that eventually create cycles. Soul ties or unholy alliances then need to be severed in order to cut a life free from spirits that are transferred and from obligations owed to such spirits.

In order to prepare for victorious life that is your inheritance, spiritual doors opened to evil influences need to be closed. It is important to pray and ask the Holy Spirit to reveal openings in our lives that welcome and entertain satanic onslaughts against the Body of Christ. Unless evil doors are shut, a believer's life is vulnerable to spiritual infections and contagious sin.

Through confession of known and unknown sin and strategic repentance, evil doors can be effectively shut to spiritual manipulation from ancestral spirits, territorial demons, and other invisible spirits seeking to compromise your life. "*If we confess our sins, He is faithful and just to forgive us our sins and to cleanse us from all unrighteousness*" (1 John 1:9). It is not His will that any should perish (see 2 Pet. 3:9).

Decree...

- I decree that every door through which the devil and his cohorts have waged demonic wars against my life, is now shut in the *heavenly realm* by the blood of Jesus and through my prayers, in Jesus' name (see Job 22:28).
- I decree that every door through which the devil and his cohorts have waged demonic wars against my life, is now

shut in the *earth realm* by the blood of Jesus and through my prayers, in Jesus' name (see Job 22:28).

- I decree that every pronouncement I have made against demonic coalitions seeking to destroy my life in accordance with:
  - Your blood (see Rev. 12:11),
  - Your word (see Isa. 55:10-11),
  - Your spirit (see John 14:17),
  - Your name (see Acts 4:12),

…will remain valid and unchallenged, in Jesus' name.

- I decree that every evil door *in the spiritual realm* through which:
  - Familiar spirits,
  - Spiritualists,
  - Witches,
  - Wizards,
  - Marine spirits,

…and other evil coalition of occultism powers have gained entrance into my life, (marriage, children's lives, business, employment, ministry, and every other relationship), is now *shut* in the name of Jesus and by the power of the blood of Jesus.

- I decree that every evil door *in the natural realm* through which:
  - Familiar spirits,
  - Spiritualists,
  - Witches,
  - Wizards,
  - Marine spirits,

...and other evil coalition of occultism powers have gained entrance into my life, (marriage, children's lives, business, employment, ministry, and every other relationship), is now shut in the name of Jesus and by the power of the blood of Jesus.

- I decree that the enemy *shall not cross the bloodline* (blood of Jesus) around my life, my husband/wife's life, children's lives, ministry, business, employment, college, in Jesus' name.

PRAYER SECTION 13

Spiritual Enemies

DESTROY SATANIC AGENTS

I had an awesome experience during 1993 when the hand of the Lord picked me up and journeyed me to a place of safety in the heavenly realm. I believe my spirit was called up as a *witness*. I was to receive training for a later date, which included watching a spirit being, a principality that was at the time already in operation on the earth. It was being invoked in an identity relevant to its demonic assignment. A deadly illness known as the HIV/Aids virus was being called up as a *familiar spirit* to make a second-round attack. I watched as the demon spirit was called up to take up a role affecting thousands of people.

Spiritual Wickedness in High Places

In a building that looked like a diagnostic center or a medical clinic, the spirit, Aids, walked out of its wooden cubicle in the form of a robotic man. When I asked to know the identity of the tall, lanky man I had seen emerge from the wooden cubicle, the Lord identified him as "HIV/Aids."

He was being invoked by the devil to attack unsuspecting victims. He would do so in the specific identity of the disease known as the HIV/Aids virus, a disease from the pits of hell. The Aids virus is an agent of destruction, and some believe, of judgment. However, regardless of public opinion, I believe the familiar spirit recycling its lifespan ought not to be tolerated by the prophetic Church who should discern its agenda.

I would suggest that Aids is simply an accusation of the enemy in the form of a deadly virus invoked against people living a lifestyle opposite to God's preordained will. Because Aids affects even heterosexual persons, I would prefer not to view this disease as a type of punishment from God, but as an end-time enemy that only the Church can defeat. Rebellion to God exposes man to the devil's attacks from familiar spirits such as HIV/Aids or new releases of demon spirits launching fresh attacks. I sincerely believe our God, being the compassionate God He is, does not need to afflict people with deadly diseases to convince them to become born again to Christ. The Lord's heart is longsuffering and He desires that all persons come to repentance, while knowing the saving love of Jesus Christ (see 2 Pet. 3:9).

Demonic agents, such as familiar spirits named in this section, are evil forces, some of which I have met in dreams and visions and have been privileged by the blood of Jesus to defeat in warfare. On every occasion, the blood of Jesus has withstood the enemy seeking after my destruction (see John 10:10).

As you read and pray these foundational prayers in faith, you will be inspired to new levels of faith. You will also find supernatural strength in the presence of the Lord from where you respond to spiritual battles. Studying other people's journeys amounts to indirect mentoring capable of transferring anointing with which past victories have been realized.

Declare...

- *Familiar spirits* are blinded and deafened to my destiny, by the power of the blood of Jesus. *They shall not accuse my future by lying about my past.*

Spiritual Enemies

- *Tracking spirits* are derailed from accessing my destiny, by the power of the blood of Jesus. *They will follow, but they shall not find me in the spirit or natural experience, in Jesus' name.*

- *Demonic bailiffs* are banned from my dwelling place, by the power of the blood of Jesus. *They shall not deliver their evil assignments to my home, in Jesus' name.*

- *Demonic sheriffs* are blinded by the blood of Jesus for my sake. *They shall not keep watch over my territory, in Jesus' name.*

- *Marine spirit agents* are demobilized for my sake, by the power of the blood of Jesus. *They shall not cause upheavals or interrupt the flow of divine blessings in my life, in Jesus' name.*

- *Territorial spirits* are chained to their evil devices for my sake by the power of the blood of Jesus. *They shall not perform their evil agendas against my life, in Jesus' name.*

- *Principalities and powers* are confused for my sake, by the power of the blood of Jesus. *Their craftiness shall be turned on them; their evil agents shall destroy one another, in Jesus' name.*

- *Rulers of the darkness of this age* are dethroned for my sake, by the power of the blood of Jesus. *They shall remain impotent and incoherent, unable to carry out their commands against my destiny, in Jesus' name.*

- *Witches, warlocks, and other occultists* are destroyed for my sake, by the power of the blood of Jesus. *Their babbles, enchantments, séances, and spells against me have been frustrated by the Lord, in Jesus' name.*

- *Astrologers, sorcerers, diviners, enchanters, magicians, prognosticators, and other demonic fraternities* that gather against my purpose are destroyed by the power of the blood of Jesus.

In Jesus' name I have prayed, Amen.

ATTACK EVIL ATTACKERS

Exposing Satanic Agendas

The devil affects and afflicts the earth through channels. He uses his demonic agents who attack believers in the daytime and at nighttime. I remember being warned by the Lord in 2003 of a new weapon formed against intercessors and watchmen. The devil was seeking to weaken prayers of intercessors and prayer warriors, and in order to achieve this evil intention, satanic agents were dispatched as *familiar spirits* to attack dream or revelatory channels. Satan's agenda revolved around deception.

Victims of this vicious attack would be deceived into eating *familiar foods* in dreams. I was made to understand that although the foods appeared and tasted real, they were actually witchcraft assignments intended to carry out premeditated spiritual warfare. This would be a new weapon formed against unsuspecting intercessors, primarily in the Western world, who were unfamiliar with the implication of eating in dreams. These faithful warriors were under siege set by demonic caterers. Satan's chefs were busy cooking witchcraft targeted at the choicest prophetic intercessors and apostolic warriors to weaken their prayer focus and language. Demonic waiters were eagerly serving familiar dishes to those intercessors and warriors who had not discovered the secret power of fasting.

I faced similar spiritual attacks as I wrote an important part of a book on prophecy. For five weeks, I suffered in the natural from severe influenza, while in dreams my weakened physical and spiritual states were fed all manner of food. Through the faithfulness of our God, the devil went too far one night by placing familiar food that I hated before me in a dream. The Holy Spirit fought back on my behalf. I prayed for hours, and when I sealed my prayers with an "Amen," I found myself rewriting the first three chapters of an already completed book. What was the devil after to have persisted in literally poisoning my systems? He dreaded exposure, so he tried to weaken my ability to receive revelation.

Spiritual Enemies

Hope Released

Unless the purpose of being fed in dreams can be substantiated by the revealed Word of God, then under no circumstance should such practices be seen as acceptable. Portions of food in apostolic warfare represent demonic concoctions meant for harm. The intended plan of the enemy is to attack prayer foundations by weakening your prayer life. I strongly believe this weapon of *food in dreams* was formed in 2003 with the devil's intention to put God's people to sleep and harvest evil seeds unchallenged.

Three years later, the enemy, operating through familiar spirits, started to seek harvests of evil seeds contained in witchcraft released through dream channels. Relationships were targeted on personal and corporate levels, and as a result, many experienced hurts, disappointments, accusations, and counteraccusations. Hope was attacked, but in 2006, the first message I received from the Lord came through a clear promise: *"For surely there is a hereafter, and your hope will not be cut off"* (Prov. 23:18).

Heaven is releasing hope to the Church to call on the Lord once more with faith and in faith (see Heb. 11:6). Through firm apostolic decrees, satan should lose expected harvests from evil seeds he has sowed in times past.

Declare Against Satan's Army...

- They will gather, but their gathering shall be in vain, in Jesus' name (see 2 Chron. 20).
- They will take counsel together, but their counsel shall not stand against my life, in Jesus' name (see Isa. 8:10).
- They will form their weapons, but their weapons shall not prosper against me or against the covenant of protection I have as a servant of the Lord, in Jesus' name (see Isa. 54:17).
- They will plot their schemes, but their desires for me shall turn upon them, in Jesus' name (see Isa. 54:17).

- They will devise their plans, but their evil plans shall lead them into the gallows they prepared for me, in Jesus' name (see Esther 6–7).
- They will chant; but their babbles shall not be established in my life, nor shall their words take root, in Jesus' name (see Isa. 44:24).
- They will perform their rites, but their works shall return to them in a sevenfold return-fire (see Deut. 28:7).
- They will consult their gods, but their gods shall respond to them with confusion (see 1 Kings 18, Dan. 2).
- They will come in a battle formation, but they shall turn against one another to their own destruction, in Jesus' name (see 2 Chron. 20).
- They will utter incantations, but their gods shall be struck with deafness; their evil incantations will be nullified by the blood of Jesus (see 1 Kings 18:28-29).
- They will consult their evil devices, but familiar spirits, their evil agents, will pronounce their end, in Jesus' name (see 1 Sam. 28).
- They will consult their demonic mirrors, but their end shall be the picture that is conjured up in Jesus' name.
- They will consult their tarot cards, but the result shall speak their end in Jesus' name.
- They will consult their talisman, but they shall be denied demonic energy. They shall be rendered powerless in Jesus' name.
- They will connect with their omens, but they shall be disconnected from their power source. Their omens shall become their nemesis in Jesus' name.
- They will call on the clouds for cover of their demonic activities, but the clouds shall expose them in Jesus' name.

Spiritual Enemies

- They shall will on the sun, moon, stars, and the firmament for cooperation, but the creation shall pronounce their end. The energy they desire shall be denied them in Jesus' name. Amen.

BREAK THEIR AGREEMENT

Satan understands the power of the blood of Jesus. He understands the value of blood, in general; after all, his agents belong to and function in fraternities, cults, and other secret societies that worship blood. Oaths of secrecy sworn to and signed by occultists revolve around agreements or pacts attested to by blood.

These deep secrets of demonic domains are now being handed divinely to the Lord's servants who are to equip the saints for the work of the ministry in order to understand strategies of satan's evil army. The time has come for the Church to challenge demonic covenants and other bonds of wickedness that lie at the foundation of lives of believers and provide the devil the necessary ammunition to attack. Satan lives in dread of this spiritual advancement of the Church. He knows his gates of hell are not able to prevail against a Church built on the revelation of Jesus Christ (see Matt. 16:18).

The harvest is truly plentiful with more harvesters being called out to the Lord's vineyard (see Matt. 9:37-38; Luke 10:2). Believers are now to arm themselves with necessary spiritual weapons, to challenge every satanic threat (see 2 Cor. 10:3-4).

But unless carnality and sin are destroyed in the Body of Christ, we will remain powerless before the barrage of demonic activities of our day. Encumbrances from natural lineages that have bonded believers to past idolatry need to be sorted out. Consider Abraham who could not look up to see the promise until he separated from the soul tie he had with Lot (see Gen. 13:8-11).

At the sound of the Word of God from your mouth, demonic coalitions, networks, covens, and the worldwide web through which guerrilla wars are being launched at you, your home, your organization, and your business, will be destroyed.

Declare Against Satanic Counsel...

- I thank You, Lord, for Your Word assures me that You have frustrated the signs of the babblers, and driven diviners mad for my sake, in Jesus' name (see Isa. 44:24-25).
- They will tell lies and seek my destruction, but I am assured by Your Word that evil men and women who seek my destruction shall not succeed. To their counsel I state, "[It] *shall not be so*" (Isa. 16:6b).
- They will come as a strong army against me, but they shall turn on one another, in Jesus' name (see 2 Chron. 20).
- They will come in one direction and flee in seven different ways (see Deut. 28:7).
- They will form their evil weapons, but they shall not prosper (see Isa. 54:17); for You, O Lord, have broken the staff of the wicked and the scepter of the rulers, in Jesus' name (see Isa. 14:5).
- They will take counsel together, but it will come to nothing, in Jesus' name (see Isa. 8:10).
- They will speak their words of agreement, but their counsel will not stand in their satanic courts, for God is with me (see Isa. 8:10).
- They will chant their babble, but it shall not stand nor shall it come to pass, in Jesus' name (see Isa. 7:7).

Lord, You Have Promised Me in Your Word in Isaiah 19...

- You will bring fear to Egypt. *Lord, bring fear to every Egyptian army seeking after my life* (e.g, my husband's life, my children's lives, my marriage, my business), *in Jesus' name.*
- You will cause the idols and other demonic tools, weapons, and utensils, with which they plot war and cook their evil

plans against me, to totter. *Lord, may their implements totter, in Jesus' name.*

- You will war for me against their evil schemes. *Lord, cause their demonic hearts to melt in fear of Your name, Jesus.*

Concerning the Evil Coalition That Has Risen Up to Destroy My Life, You Have Promised to...

- *"Set Egyptian against Egyptian."* Lord, let it be so, in Jesus' name.

Lord, According to Your Word in Isaiah 55:11, Which Shall not Return to You Void, You Shall...

- Set witches against witches.
- Set occultists against occultists.
- Set principality against principality.
- Set satanists against satanists.
- Set wizards against wizards.
- Set every other identity of the devil against the other (see Isa. 19:2).

Lord, I Pray in Accordance With Your Word in Isaiah 19...

- May the spirit of Egypt, which raises its voice over Your voice in my life, fail in its midst, in Jesus' name.
- May You utterly destroy the agents of Egypt that challenge Your Word in my life, in Jesus' name.
- May You overwhelm the spirit of Egypt with Your judgment as You did in the days of Pharaoh, in Jesus' name.
- May Your fire consume the supply pipelines used by the spirit of Egypt to fuel spiritual wars against my life, in Jesus' name.
- May these spirits no longer have impact on human agents used (against their will) to further the cause of evil.

- May every human under demonic influence be released from satanic arrests to seek the Lord as Savior, in Jesus' name.
- May every human deployed as a satanic agent to destroy my peace, in the night hours as well as the daytime, be set free from deception, in Jesus' name.

I Thank You, Lord, for I Have Called Upon You According to Psalm 35…

- "*Fight against those who fight against me. Take hold of shield and buckler, and stand up for my help. Also draw out the spear, and stop those who pursue me. Say to my soul, 'I am your salvation'*" (Ps. 35:1b-3).
- May my vindication come speedily from the Lord, in Jesus' name.

Lord, I Press Into Your Word in Psalm 35…

- May evil forces seeking after my life be brought to shame and dishonor, in Jesus' name.
- May evil forces plotting my hurt be turned back and brought into confusion, in Jesus' name.
- May they become like chaff before the wind, in Jesus' name.
- May the angel of the Lord pursue them, in Jesus' name.
- May their way be dark and slippery, in Jesus' name.
- May the angel of the Lord defeat them, in Jesus' name.
- May their nets, which they have hidden for me, catch them in their evil devices, in Jesus' name.
- May they fall into the same destruction they have wished me, in Jesus' name (see Ps. 35:4-8).

Amen!

PRAYER SECTION 14

Engage With Angelic Forces

We are to partner with angels who have been given to the Church to serve us. Daniel, the great man of prayer and revelation, partnered with the angelic hosts (see Dan. 9–10), so did John, the Revelator (see Rev. 1). Peter was released from jail by an angel of the Lord (see Acts 12), while Joshua saw the angel as the Commander of God's army (see Josh. 5:13-15). In addition, the angel of the Lord visited Gideon to commission him for his ministry as a deliverer (see Judg. 6:11). As the Church advances in her end-time mandate and pressure mounts in hell with manifestation of evil increasing in our midst, believers in Christ Jesus are also to engage with angelic activities. We must learn to partner with the angelic host in this apostolic age.

Declare...

- May angels be released to me to give me skills to understand how I must pray.

- May the angels of the Lord join me in seeking out evil men who plot against my destiny (see Ps. 94:5-6).
- May announcing angels be positioned to announce the defeat of those who come against God's ordained will for my life.
- May the angels of the Lord uphold God's judgment against workers of evil that attack my life.
- May heavenly helicopters be dispatched in search of workers of iniquity—evil destroyers who gather against my purpose in the night hours.
- May angelic intelligence officers be released against those who gather to destroy me and my family (see Rev. 12:7).
- May those who gather against me gather in vain and their plans be aborted by the blood of Jesus (see Ps. 91).
- May every prince of Persia hindering divine messengers assigned for my benefit be destroyed by the fire of the Holy Ghost (see Dan. 10:13).
- May every prince of Greece assigned to challenge my divine messengers, bow and be destroyed by the fire of the Holy Ghost (see Dan. 10:20).
- I command the land I have been posted to—[name your area]—as a watchman to deny access to demonic agents (see Ps. 125:3).
- I command the gates of my city to be shut to demonic invisible travelers, enchanters, sorcerers, witches, wizards, chanters, diviners, and other occultists (see Gen. 22:17).
- I release my prophetic voice to awaken righteous intercessors and watchmen to stand in the gap for my life and my city, in Jesus' name (see Ezek. 22:30).
- I decree that every spirit I have bound as I pray shall be bound in Heaven, in Jesus' name (see Matt. 16:19).

Amen.

According to Your Word in Isaiah 7:7, Evil Forces Have Gathered to Plot Their Schemes Against My Life and My Family to…

- Trouble us.
- To cause us division.
- To cause distraction.
- To rule over our home, life, and work.

But You have promised, Lord: "It shall not stand, nor shall it come to pass" (Isa. 7:7b).

Lord, let it be so, in Jesus' name.

PRAYER SECTION 15

Evil Communication Systems

I am particularly fond of the prayer in this section because the heart of it made so much sense to me when the Holy Spirit taught me to pray it. I had confronted a person I believed was operating in witchcraft after watching patterns and sequences with which every person around them mysteriously fell ill with near-death experiences or ghastly car crashes, including me. While it is fine to be nice and loving to those around you, you must not be ignorant over affairs entrusted in your hands.

How is a manager of human resources able to manage if he is not aware of how many employees are in his care? Or how does a housekeeper account for a house if he has not taken inventory of its contents? I was living my life under the same delusion as many other believers, thinking the devil was out there somewhere, but not being entirely sure where. I was under a heart and mind bondage that prevented me from interpreting genuine Holy Spirit-inspired thought. Consequently, for a long time, the devil operated from close range

Evil Communication Systems

within our church buildings, amongst our congregations, to the point where we had so-called believers who never spoke an establishing "Amen." The Body of Christ has become infiltrated with demonic agents masking as believers in Christ who are not really in church to establish, but to destroy righteous foundations.

Shortly after the Lord taught me to pray against the enemy's communication systems, a friend shared a profound dream she had. In the dream, the enemy presented in the form of a chef in a restaurant who presented her with a mobile telephone handset. As the man was trying to give the handset to her, it fell on the restaurant floor and broke open. She said she was shocked as she saw in the memory of the telephone, names and telephone numbers of key Christian leaders, including her own Christian friends. At the same time, a few people we knew started experiencing bizarre instances where telephone numbers dialed would ring through to strange numbers. Equally absurd was the fact that the telephone screen would show the right number and name, but the voice at the other end of the telephone would be someone totally different. When I experienced this same thing, I understood the message of Heaven—a communication war was about to break out.

It is important to allow the Holy Spirit to teach you a new language of prayer. I remember the Lord also teaching me to call in prayer for the appropriate weapon in any spiritual warfare. In other words, every war has weapons suited to the nature of the aggression. If an enemy's communication systems are destroyed, then their battle formation will certainly go into confusion bringing disorientation and eventually surrender.

Destroy Demonic Communication Systems...

- Lord, I command angels of the Lord, which are assigned to my city, region, and nation, to converge for the sake of the believers.
- I command the angels of the Lord to comb through spiritual soils of my city to uproot every negative word spoken by persons (especially those in authority over my life

or persons claiming authority of my life), now arming satanic agents.

- I command angels of the Lord to deny access to demonic forces to any words spoken carelessly against me. *Negative words spoken will no longer strengthen the devil and his cohorts working against my purpose.*

- I command angels of the Lord to join me in declaring negative words working against my life inoperative, their powers nullified by the blood of Jesus.

- I command the angelic hosts to tie the tongues of those who utter evil judgments, incantations, or pronounce spells against my life. *May such words be negated by the blood of Jesus, their power made null and void in the spiritual realms, in Jesus' name.*

- I command the angels of the Lord to intercept and interrupt every evil communication against my life, and to prevent that communication from being transmitted by land, telephone, mobile telephone, email, instant messaging, paging, television, newsprint, or any other means of communication, in Jesus' name.

- I command the angelic hosts to obliterate any evil communication, written or not, against me. *May every charge sheet in hell working against me be destroyed by the power of the blood of Jesus.*

- I command the angelic hosts to destroy any sound communication and to nullify any typed words or images communicating evil missions against myself, my family, my ministry, and my business, in Jesus' name. *May such images of me and my family be destroyed in Jesus' name.*

- I command the angelic hosts to demobilize and destroy evil surveillance systems with which demonic eyes spy on my life and that of others around me, in Jesus' name.

Evil Communication Systems

- I command the angelic hosts to destroy demonic communication links, communication masts, and other devices through which evil eyes communicate warfare agendas against my life, in Jesus' name.
- I command the angelic hosts to detect and destroy every demonic hotspot through which demonic assignments are communicated in my neighborhood, in Jesus' name.
- I command the angelic hosts to detect and destroy all other feeder transmission links through which evil forces monitor my life and that of my family's, in Jesus' name.
- I command the angelic hosts to terrorize every spiritual terrorist and to destroy spiritual terrorist camps (such as witches' covens) that support warfare strategies against my life, my family, ministry, and business, in Jesus' name.
- I command angels to frustrate evil recruiting devices with which demonic associations establish themselves in my spiritual climate.
- I command the angelic hosts to shut every gateway into the souls of people weakened by sin and rebellion from demonic manipulation.

In Jesus' name.

PRAYER SECTION 16

Present-Day Wars of the Church

The global Church of Christ is experiencing birth pangs at present in preparation for the birthing of the glorious apostolic Church. God questioned Isaiah, *"Shall I bring to the time of birth, and not cause delivery?"* (Isa. 66:9a).

The Church is encountering new enemies in the 21st century, such as humanism, Islam, secularism, and other ideologies. Subsequently, the Church, being the Bride of Christ, needs to engage more with her destiny as the glorious Church that Christ laid His life down for. It is our responsibility to make the manifold wisdom of Christ known to principalities and powers in the heavenly places (see Eph. 3:10).

It is possible for an enemy to become a friend, but it is impossible for satan and his cohorts to ever be anything but an adversary. During this time of combat or warfare, your responsibility is to cast out evil—not to minister to evil. Believers must not allow evil to root in their homes and lives, for it will contaminate, multiply, and overcome us. For instance, so many Western societies are being bullied to accept the minority voices of homosexuality and Islam. Long-term consequences of short-term conveniences appear not to matter. So, what should Christians do?

The Bible warns of the evil of the last days, and numerous Scriptures warn Christian believers of *"such a time as this"* (see Esther 4:14b). As children of the living God, we do not repay evil with evil but by destroying the works of evil. Humans who are bonded to evil or bound by spiritual wickedness deserve to be set free from deception. But unless you and other believers rise up to confront spiritual wickedness in high places, demonic voices will continue to influence affairs of life from politics to economy.

Pray…

- Lord, I bless and glorify Your name. I thank You for shedding Your blood at Calvary for my salvation and freedom. I thank You, Lord, for I have not been given the spirit of fear, but of love, of power, and of a sound mind. Fear will not have dominion over me. So I call upon Your name with confidence and faith. I know You are near to those that call upon You. Deliver me, O Lord, from evil and preserve my soul from destruction.

- I commend my struggles into Your hands and trust in Your ability to war against any evil, oppressive influences affecting my life.

- Teach me, Lord, to take responsibility for my life by paying heed to Your Word. Teach me, Lord, to be a praying Christian and one whose faith is anchored in You. Help me, Lord, to worship Your majesty. May the worship of Your name defeat every evil presence affecting my life and propel me into my destiny to serve You. In Jesus' name, Amen.

Praying Against Witchcraft

The Word of God commands in the Old Testament: "*You shall not permit a sorceress to live*" (Exod. 22:18). Some in the Body of Christ believe witches should be allowed to live, which seems to be in total opposition to this Scripture found in Exodus. The reason for their argument is based on the dispensation of grace. Furthermore, it is important to be reminded that the Ten Commandments given to Moses in the Old Testament include, "Thou shall not kill." Yet in the same dispensation, the Bible warned of the fate of one who practiced witchcraft. Jesus Christ warned that He did not come to destroy the Law, or the prophets, referring to the Old Testament. Rather, He said, "*I did not come to destroy but to fulfill*" (Matt. 5:17b). Old Testament Scriptures are not to be seen as outdated but as new in Christ, who is the fulfillment of the Old. In a way, Jesus Christ made sense of the Old Testament by fulfilling every word that was written.

It would be considered illegal to murder any person for any reason, including witchcraft. Rather, spirits behind the witchcraft should be cursed with the Word of God. Cursing a spirit carries the same weight as death because its influence is not expected to manifest thereafter. To effectively pray against witchcraft, certain requirements have to be met. It is important to separate spirits behind witchcraft and individuals whose compromised lives serve as channels for witchcraft or other forms of occultism. By cursing spirits behind the witchcraft, those who practice the act still have hope for salvation. The dispensation of grace offers all men a free gift of salvation by virtue of the sacrifice of His life (see John 3:16). Those who continue to reject this offer are "sons of perdition."

Ancestral Witchcraft

The Bible defines *rebellion* as akin to witchcraft; however, there are more dangerous forms of witchcraft, some of which have invaded the church.

Ancestral witchcraft is practiced by individuals who might have become possessed by the ruling demonic agents responsible for maintaining allegiance to family idols. These invisible spirit beings also hold responsibility for distributing demonic assignments. Often, after midnight, persons initiated into ancestral witchcraft may no longer possess control of their natural senses. In obedience, the watch of the enemy is kept by his followers whose evil powers are most potent between 12 midnight and 3:00 a.m. In the particular case that I observed, as well as other incidents I have read about, persons bound in witchcraft target people closest to them. Acting like out-of-control vehicles, they play games with marriages, destinies, children, and every benefit a Christian is to enjoy. And until harassed with apostolic prayer, practitioners of witchcraft and black magic continually raise the stakes in a ploy to shut down Christian activities. Bringing death to a witch should not be seen as literal murder, which would be a criminal case, but as burying evil powers from where principalities draw their strength. This is the only prescription for witchcraft annulment; and the only way to release the spirit of any person under such oppression is to attack with revelation spirits resident in their lives.

Present Your Case

The Lord does not honor judgmental words spoken against another person, nor will prayers based on suspicion carry weight in Heaven. However, when confronting the use of idols in Israel, God said, "*'Present your case,' says the Lord, 'Bring forth your strong reasons,' says the King of Jacob*" (Isa. 41:21). Demonic influences are powerless before a praying Christian.

- Lord, I come in the power of Your precious blood and Your Word in Micah 5:12, which promises me that You will cut off sorceries from my hand. *Lord, may Your Word be established in my life, in Jesus' name.*

- Lord, Your Word promises me in Numbers 23:23a: "*For there is no sorcery against Jacob, nor any divination against Israel.*" There is therefore no sorcery against me, nor any divination against my life, for I am blessed of the Lord.

Lord, I Now Pray…

- May the chanting of evil forces against the righteous lead to their destruction, for You have said in Your Word, "*Do not touch My anointed ones, and do My prophet no harm"* (Ps. 105:15b).

- May their decreeing (evil pronouncements) fall to the ground, in Jesus' name (see Isa. 54:17).
- May their words, forecasts, spells, predictions return to them void and empty; without the evil result they desire, in Jesus' name (see Isa. 8:10).
- May their witchcraft brooms, spell books, demonic mirrors, tarot cards, and crystal balls used against me or any other believer bring them confusion, in Jesus' name (see Dan. 2).
- May the demonic identities with which they astral travel, astral project to conduct evil missions be arrested and sent back to hell, in Jesus' name.
- May their evil communication devices broadcast their own destruction, in Jesus' name (see Isa. 7:7).
- May they rise but fall in their own destruction, in Jesus' name (see Isa. 41:12).
- May those who use evil identities be unmasked, and may their lives surrender to the saving power of Jesus Christ, in Jesus' name.

Thank You, Lord for Your promise to Your children which says, *"You shall seek them and not find them—those who contended with you. Those who war against you shall be as nothing, as a nonexistent thing"* (Isa. 41:12).

PRAYER SECTION 17

God Has a Hedge Around You

For sometime I had heard messages preached about God's faithfulness, but never realized that I was not connecting with the reality of what I was hearing. It was not until a few years ago when an invited speaker to an event I was organizing was unable to attend, that the Lord then challenged me to teach on the benefits of His blood sacrifice. My mind-set was radically shifted when I realized how privileged I was as a beneficiary of irrevocable promises. One strong promise set in the covenant every born-again believer has with the Lord is of divine protection from evil (see Isa. 54:17). Since my experience, I have come to believe in spiritual hedges around my life and the lives of others. The devil is unable to challenge destinies of faithful believers without permission from the Lord. The Bible makes this fact clear:

> To turn aside the justice due a man before the face of the Most High, or subvert a man in his cause—the Lord does not approve. Who is he who speaks and it comes to pass, when the Lord has not commanded it? (Lamentations 3:35-37)

Job's experience provides credence to my viewpoint. Before Job's gruelling experience, to say the least, God showed him off to satan as an upright man. Typically, satan set off to accuse Job: *"Does Job fear God for nothing? Have you not made a hedge around him, around his household, and around all that he has on every side?"* (Job 1:9b-10a).

You might already know it, but God also has a hedge of protection around you and all that concerns you. But in order to call on the Lord uncompromisingly, especially in times of trouble, you need to break bonds of wickedness in your life. A holy God can receive petitions only from persons walking in purity. I remember receiving revelation that set me free in areas of understanding where I was bound by fear. I was reliably informed by the Holy Spirit that nothing could ever happen to me on earth without the Lord's knowledge. In other words, satan is unable to harm or kill me because he is not allowed to—a fact confirmed in the Word of God: *"'No weapon formed against you shall prosper, and every tongue which rises against you in judgment you shall condemn. This is the heritage of the servants of the Lord, and their righteousness is from Me,' says the Lord"* (Isa. 54:17).

The word "heritage" in the Scripture above means "inheritance." So, in other words, it is your inheritance to serve the Lord free of demonic missiles. Satan was envious of Job's right standing with God, so he questioned God concerning Job: *"Have you not made a hedge around him, around his household, and around all that he has on every side?"* (Job 1:10a). Satan was afraid of the hedge of protection God had placed around Job, just as he is afraid of the hedge Jesus has established around you by His blood. The blood of Jesus offers continuous protection from satanic harassments, oppressions, and the ever-increasing cosmic turmoil. These demonic forces are converging across the earth in strong coalitions in readiness for epic battles with apostolic warriors. However, a radical praying army is being released across the earth with the heart of Gideon to dethrone satanic rule in the hearts of men and in lands. Radical holiness and obedience will be the protection of this army who will be determined to execute God's judgment in the land of the living.

Pray...

- I thank You, Lord, for every hedge of protection around my life (see Job 1:10).
- I thank You, Lord, for being the wall of fire around my life (see Zech. 2:5).
- I thank You, Lord, for making me like Mt. Zion, which cannot be moved but which shall endure forever (see Ps. 125:1).
- I thank You, Lord, for Your "watch" over my life; if You be for me, who can be against me? (see Ps. 127:1; Rom. 8:31).
- I thank You, Lord, for making me a fortified city and an iron pillar (see Jer. 1:18).
- I thank You, Lord, for making me like a deer, to walk in my high places (see Hab. 3:19).
- I thank You, Lord, for making me fearless; Your fear alone I shall covet (see Ps. 27:3).
- I thank You, Lord, that my times are in Your hands so I shall be anxious for nothing (see Phil. 4:6).
- I thank You, Lord, for being my Shepherd; I shall not want, nor shall I fear evil (see Ps. 23).
- I thank You, Lord, for answered prayers (see Isa. 65:24).

In Jesus' name, Amen.

Every war waged by satan against you begins in the mind where he seeks to lodge his lies. Satan's evil devices are intended to frustrate your faith; hence, you are to fight back (see Heb. 11:6). Spiritual strength is drawn from understanding your covenant right and inheritance in God. Spiritual wars should be engaged in with a mind-set of victory. They are to be perceived as opportunities to make *"the manifold wisdom of God...known by the church to the principalities and powers in the heavenly places"* (Eph. 3:10).

PRAYER SECTION 18

Releasing Divine Blessings

OPEN NEW DIVINE DOORS

The creative Word of God is in your mouth to re-create any situation from negative to positive. It is important, therefore, for you to declare the Word of God and to prophesy your new beginnings. The Bible encourages us to speak with confidence and expectancy, and God's Word declared out of your mouth will be established for you when you speak in faith (see Job 22:28).

Satan relishes the gaps and openings that give him access into lives of those he wishes to attack. These gaps are created if your heart is not filled with the Word of God. Satan, being the cunning, deceitful serpent he is, will try to fill any vacuum in your life with lies and deceit as he did with Adam. His aim is to set up thrones of iniquity from where he controls and manipulates his victim.

Often, believers labor in prayer to evict negative influences, such as bad financial records, from their lives. However, unless righteous foundations of financial prudence are set, the enemy will attempt to lure such people back into debt. You are the temple of the living God, designed to serve as a dwelling place for the Almighty (see 1 Cor. 3:16-19). Righteous perspectives ought to direct hearts into godly endeavors.

Pray...

- I decree my boundaries are out of bounds to demonic coalitions, regiments, and hierarchies, in Jesus' name.

And as such...

- I decree that my new divine doors of freedom, liberty, joy, good health, sound mind, boldness, prosperity, favor, promotion, and fruitfulness are open, and will stay open forever, in Jesus' name.

- I decree that my new divine doors of favor are now open to me, in Jesus' name. I shall walk in divine favor to fulfill my destiny (see Esther 5:3).

- I decree my new divine doors of freedom are now open to me, in Jesus' name. I shall walk in freedom in Christ to achieve my divine purpose, in Jesus' name (see John 8:36).

- I decree my new divine doors of prosperity are now open to me. I shall walk in supernatural blessing, in Jesus' name (see 3 John 1:2).

- I decree my new divine doors of good health are now open. I shall walk in fullness of health to accomplish my goals, in Jesus' name (see Isa. 53:5).

- I decree my new divine doors of promotion are now open. I shall walk in the elevation of the Lord to fulfill my purpose, in Jesus' name (see Ps. 118:20).

- I decree my new divine doors of business are now open in Jesus' name. I receive supernatural power (see Ps. 68:9-11), and I receive the power to make wealth in Jesus' name (see Deut. 8:18).

- I decree my divine doors of financial breakthrough are now open. I shall walk in divine riches in Jesus' name. I now welcome my ship of Tarshish to unload my wealth. I welcome kings and princes to deliver the wealth of their nations, in Jesus' name (see Isa. 60).
- I decree my new divine doors of fruitfulness are now open, in Jesus' name. I shall be fruitful and I shall multiply, in Jesus' name (see Gen. 1:28).
- I decree my new divine doors of joy are now open, in Jesus' name. I shall rejoice, and laughter shall fill my mouth, in Jesus' name (see Ps. 16:11).
- I decree my new divine doors of strategic relationships are now open. I shall enjoy fruitful partnerships for sake of the Kingdom of Heaven, in Jesus' name (see Esther 9:29).
- I decree my new divine doors of ministry are now open. I have overcome every adversary of my destiny, and I shall serve the Lord with all my heart, in Jesus' name (see 1 Cor. 16:9).

RELEASING DIVINE BLESSING

I Declare...

- *I shall not be **barren**;* for the Word of God assures me *that there shall be no barren in the land* (see Deut. 7:14). I shall carry good seeds in my natural and spiritual wombs to full term, in Jesus' name.
- *I shall not suffer from **misplacements***, for the Word of God assures me that I shall not build and then another inhabit; I shall not plant and another eat (see Isa. 65:22). I shall enjoy the fruit of my labor, in Jesus' name.
- *I shall not suffer from **miscarriage of purpose***, for the Word of God assures me of God's thoughts toward me; they are thoughts of peace and not of evil, to give me a future and a hope (see Jer. 29:11).

- *I shall not suffer from **insomnia**,* for the Word of God assures me that "*He gives His beloved sleep*" (Ps. 127:2b). I shall enjoy my rest, in Jesus' name.

- *I shall not suffer from **lack**,* for the Word of God assures me that I am "*blessed…with every spiritual blessing in the heavenly places in Christ*" (Eph. 1:3b). I shall enjoy my covenant blessings, in Jesus' name.

- *I shall not suffer **despair**,* for the Word of God declares that the hope of the righteous shall not be cut off (see Prov. 23:18). I shall walk in hope and assurance in the Lord's promises, in Jesus' name.

- *I shall not suffer from **fear**,* for the Word of God assures me, "*For God has not given us a spirit of fear, but of power and of love and of a sound mind*" (2 Tim. 1:7). I shall serve the Lord in confidence and boldness, in Jesus' name.

- *I shall not suffer from **confusion**,* for the Word of God assures me that "*we have the mind of Christ*" (1 Cor. 2:16b).

- *I shall not suffer from **stress**,* for the Word of God assures me "*Peace I leave with you, My peace I give to you*" (John 14:27a). I shall live with the peace of the Lord, in Jesus' name.

- *I shall not suffer from **isolation**,* for the Word of God assures me, "*But I have called you friends, for all things that I heard from My Father I have made known to you*" (John 15:15b). I shall live in the confidence of God's presence with me, in Jesus' name.

- *I shall not suffer from **loneliness**,* for the Word of God assures me, "*But the Helper, the Holy Spirit, whom the Father will send in My name, He will teach you all things, and bring to your remembrance all things that I said to you*" (John 14:26).

- *I shall not suffer from **anxiety**,* for the Word of God assures me, "*Be anxious for nothing*" (Phil. 4:6a). I shall make my requests known to the Lord by prayer and supplications, and with thanksgiving, in Jesus' name.

- *I shall not suffer from* **deprivation**, for the Word of God assures me that my God *"daily loads us with benefits"* (Ps. 68:19b).
- *I shall not suffer from* **diseases and infirmity**, for the Word of God assures me *"By His stripes we are healed"* (Isa. 53:5b).
- *I shall not suffer from* **drought**, for the Word of God assures me, *"The Lord will...satisfy your soul in drought"* (Isa. 58:11a).
- *I shall not suffer from* **hair loss**, for the Word of God assures me that He knows the number of hairs on my head (see Matt. 10:30).
- *I shall not suffer from* **discouragement** for the Word of God commands me to *"Rejoice in the Lord always. Again I will say, rejoice!"* (Phil. 4:4).
- *I shall not suffer from* **demonic oppression**, for the Word of God assures me, *"No weapon formed against you shall prosper"* (Isa. 54:17a).
- *I shall not suffer from* **tongues of men** nor suffer from effects of gossip and slander, for the Word of God assures me, *"Every tongue which rises against you in judgment you shall condemn"* (Isa. 54:17b).
- *I shall not suffer from* **lukewarmness**, for the Word of God assures me He makes His ministers *"a flame of fire"* (Ps. 104:4b).
- *I shall not suffer from* **premature death**, for the Word of God assures me *"with long life I will satisfy him"* (Ps. 91:16).
- *I shall not suffer from* **ignorance**, for the Word of God assures me, *"Let this mind be in you which was also in Christ Jesus"* (Phil. 2:5).

- *I shall not suffer from **weariness**,* for the Word of God assures me, *"Those who wait on the Lord shall renew their strength; they shall mount up with wings like eagles, they shall run and not be weary, they shall walk and not faint"* (Isa. 40:31).

In Jesus' name.

Bibliography

Eckhardt, John. *Moving in the Apostolic*. Ventura, CA: Renew Books, 1999.

Nwankpa, Emeka. *Idolatry*. Accra, Ghana: Rehoboth Publishing, 2004.

Pax-Harry, Obii. *Prophetic Engagement-Issachar Mandate*. Italy: Destiny Image Europe, 2006.

Pierce, Chuck D. and Sytsema, Rebecca Wagner. *The Future War of the Church*. Ventura, CA: Renew Books, 2001.

Scott, Martin. *Sowing Seeds for Revival*. Tonbridge, Kent: Sovereign World, 2001.

Sherrer, Quin and Garlock, Ruthanne. *A Woman's Guide To Breaking Bondages*. Annarbor, MI: Servant Publications, 1994.

Wagner, C. Peter. *Breaking Strongholds in Your City*. Ventura, CA: Regal Books, 1997.

Wagner, C. Peter, ed. *Confronting the Powers*. Tonbridge, Kent: Sovereign World, 1996.

Wagner, C. Peter. *Territorial Spirits*. Tonbridge, Kent: Sovereign World, 1991.

Wentroble, Barbara. *A People of Destiny*. Colorado Springs, CO: Wagner Publications, 2000.

Contact the Author

PAST. OBII PAX-HARRY

E-mail:
metanoia60@aol.com

Websites:
www.womenarisepray.org
www.rlachurch.org

Winner of the 2006 Fred Grossmith Christian Writer's Award for non-fiction (Bronze)

PROPHETIC ENGAGEMENT, THE ISSACHAR MANDATE

Unlocking the Hidden Power of the Interpretive Function in the Gift of Prophecy

By Obii Pax-Harry

And this Gospel of the Kingdom shall be preached in all the world for a witness unto all nations; and then shall the end come (Matthew 24:14).

Now is the time to reach out and share God with the world. Using the gifts He gave you will bring about His purpose in your life—and the Church as a whole.

Prophetic Engagement is a "clarion call" to the prophetic church to:

- ◆ Reposition the gift of prophecy to an interpretative role.
- ◆ Engage more proactively with Christian media.
- ◆ Serve the unsaved world with divine abilities granted by God.
- ◆ Establish an apostolic and prophetic Christian media army.
- ◆ Set firm foundations so the house of God can stand as designed.

Learn today how you can move the Gospel forward!

ISBN-13: 978-88-89127-31-5

Order Now from Destiny Image Europe
Telephone: +39 085 4716623- Fax +39 085 4716622
E-mail: ordini@eurodestinyimage.com

Internet: www.eurodestinyimage.com

Additional copies of this book and other book titles from DESTINY IMAGE EUROPE are available at your local bookstore.

We are adding new titles every month!

To view our complete catalog on-line, visit us at:
www.eurodestinyimage.com

Send a request for a catalog to:

Via Acquacorrente, 6
65123 - Pescara - ITALY
Tel. +39 085 4716623 - Fax +39 085 4716622

"Changing the world, one book at a time."

Are you an author?

Do you have a "today" God-given message?

CONTACT US

We will be happy to review your manuscript for a possible publishing:

publisher@eurodestinyimage.com